COVERS OF
THE SATURDAY
EVENING POST

Norman Rockwell
MAY 29, 1926

COVERS OF
THE SATURDAY
EVENING POST

SEVENTY YEARS OF OUTSTANDING ILLUSTRATION
FROM AMERICA'S FAVORITE MAGAZINE

TEXT BY
JAN COHN

DESIGN BY JOSEPH RUTT

SMITHMARK

COVERS OF THE SATURDAY EVENING POST text by Jan Cohn.
Copyright© Curtis Archives, Inc., a division of the Curtis Publishing Company, 1995. Reprinted by
arrangement with Penguin Studio Books, a division of Penguin Books USA Inc.

This edition published in 1998 by SMITHMARK Publishers,
a division of U.S. Media Holdings, Inc.,
115 West 18th Street, New York, NY 10011.

SMITHMARK Books are available for bulk purchase for sales promotion and premium use.
For details write or call the manager of special sales, SMITHMARK Publishers,
115 West 18th Street, New York, NY 10011.

ISBN: 0-7651-9114-8

Printed in Hong Kong

10 9 8 7 6 5 4 3 2 1

Library of Congress Cataloging-in-Publication Data

Cohn, Jan, 1933-
     Covers of the Saturday evening post: seventy years of outstanding
     illustration from America's favorite magazine/text by Jan Cohn;
     design by Joseph Rutt.
          p. cm.
     Originally published: New York: Viking, 1995.
     Includes index.
     ISBN 0-7651-9114-8
     1. Saturday evening post. 2. Magazine covers--United States.
     I. Rutt, Joseph. II. Title.
     NC974.4.S28C64   1998
     741.6'52'0973--dc21   98-13627
                                                              CIP

To the publishers of the *Saturday Evening Post:*

Cyrus H. Curtis,
under whose leadership the first *Post* cover appeared;

Cory and Beurt SerVaas,
for their tireless efforts to preserve and
maintain the rich heritage of the *Saturday Evening Post*

ACKNOWLEDGMENTS

This record of the covers of the *Saturday Evening Post* is created out of the work of hundreds of persons who, starting nearly a century ago, dressed up a struggling new weekly magazine with a first-page, full-page illustration. Such a record must certainly acknowledge first the artists themselves, the men and women whose work is reproduced here, all of whom, in one way or another, painted a version of American life. Beyond the artists themselves, there were the editors and art editors, the engravers and the printers, who were responsible for turning those vivid representations of America into the covers themselves, mass-produced in the millions and distributed every Tuesday throughout the country.

This collection of the covers of the *Post* has itself been several years in the making, and could not have been undertaken or completed without the contributions of a number of dedicated people, especially those in Indianapolis, at The Curtis Publishing Company and the *Saturday Evening Post*. Thanks must go to Joan SerVaas Durham, president of The Curtis Publishing Company, for her vision and presentation of the idea for the book to Viking Studio Books. A thank you also to part of the staff at Curtis, Sheri McKain, Cristy Hilgemeier, and Sheila Kavanagh, for their diligence and hard work in gathering and assembling the materials needed to create a book that spans seven decades.

In writing the text to accompany the reproduced covers of the *Post*, I found myself, once again, deeply indebted to Carol N. Brown of The Curtis Publishing Company. Her deep and broad knowledge of the *Post* and of the illustrators who created the covers has been invaluable. Thanks, too, to Martha Schueneman, my editor at Viking Studio Books; Viking Studio's publisher, Michael Fragnito, who saw the potential of this book; and Roni Axelrod, Cindy Achar, Bitite Vinklers, and Joseph Rutt, whose skills and talents combined to produce and design this book. And a word of gratitude is appropriate as well to the new Norman Rockwell Museum in Stockbridge, Massachusetts, where I had the opportunity to examine closely some of Rockwell's original cover paintings.

Jan Cohn
Hartford, Connecticut

CONTENTS

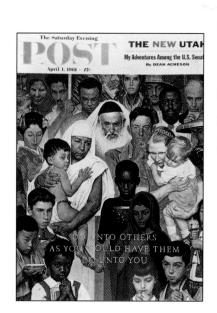

Norman Rockwell
MARCH 9, 1929

INTRODUCTION

The old saw that you can't tell a book by its cover does not hold true for magazines. A quick survey of any newsstand demonstrates that each magazine's cover is an announcement of that magazine's identity. Expensive magazines for upscale readers present "quiet" covers. Those intended for a wider market are typically noisier with both color and text; like an old-fashioned dime-store window, they advertise through clutter.

Graphics and text, layout and color choices combine to serve a complex function. The name of the magazine, the logo, and the general graphic style carry over from issue to issue, guaranteeing the loyal reader continuity. At the same time, each cover offers something new, with brief blurbs promising exciting articles and stories.

Whatever the variations, most modern magazines use art as their centerpiece. This may be a photograph, a line drawing, or a painting; it may depict a beautiful woman, a fancy dessert, or a caricature of a famous person. This piece of art is a magazine's major statement, and it is not chosen at random. In subject and style, the cover art, like the title and the logo, conveys the "idea" of the magazine.

This book salutes a great American magazine, and, appropriately, it honors that magazine through a retrospective of its covers. Middle-of-the-road, middlebrow, and middle class, the *Saturday Evening Post* long claimed the largest audience of any magazine, indeed of any mass medium, in the nation. The greatness of the *Post* was rooted in how accurately it reflected American life. In the fiction and articles it printed, in its editorials, even in the advertisements that swelled its pages, the *Post* provided Americans with a weekly mirror in which to see themselves. For its covers, the *Saturday Evening Post* found the illustrators to translate that reflection of our national life into pictures.

What is best remembered today of the old *Post* is its covers, and what is best remembered of those covers is the work of the magazine's most famous cover artist, Norman Rockwell. But Rockwell was not alone; in the great period of American illustration, almost all the finest illustrators of the day contributed art for the *Post*'s cover. A list of these illustrators includes such names as J. C. Leyendecker, Harrison Fisher, Charles Livingston Bull, James Montgomery Flagg, Stevan Dohanos, and many, many more.

Post covers offered a variety of cheerful visions of American life. There were portraits—of beautiful women, comical children, rural oldsters, famous personages. There were narrative covers, and without doubt telling American stories in pictures was Norman Rockwell's greatest contribution. There were topical covers, particularly during the two World Wars, and nature covers that featured animals, mountain vistas, and rural landscapes. There were covers to celebrate holidays, from Christmas to the Fourth of July, and covers to record the variety and vitality of the American scene. Over the decades, *Post* covers changed, bringing new subject matter, new artists, and new graphic styles to millions of readers. A history of these covers, from black-and-white line drawings to four-color photographs, is in itself a mini-history of American illustration.

The *Post* and its covers have become such an important a part of the history of American popular culture that it comes as something of a surprise to discover that the magazine once had no cover at all. When Cyrus Curtis bought the near-defunct *Saturday Evening Post* for $1,000 in August 1897, it was in need of every kind of resuscitation. And Curtis did set about immediate reforms, including an urgently needed facelift—though nothing so cosmetically extreme as a separate cover. Although contemporary monthly magazines appeared with staid covers, the *Post* was still closer to a weekly tabloid, and for the time being it was adequate to clean up the type face, improve the first-page layout, and experiment with a variety of ways to present the logo.

The *Post* cover developed gradually. Improving of the visual elements of the magazine included introducing artwork, both illustrations and ornamentation, and the most important of these appeared on the first page. But such art remained subordinate to the text until the spring of 1899, when on the first page of the May 27 issue, commemorating what was then called Decoration Day (now Memorial Day), a boxed poem, "The Fallen of the Fight," by Frank L. Stanton, and an appropriate illustration appeared with equal importance.

Two weeks later, Cyrus Curtis made his most important decision for the *Saturday Evening Post*. On June 10, 1899, he named George Horace Lorimer editor; Lorimer, one of America's preeminent magazine editors, held this position through 1936. During the first summer, he worked to prove himself and his magazine, searching out important articles and fiction, soliciting advertising, and experimenting with the artwork and layout of page one.

Sometimes the text took the greater amount of space; at other times, it appeared in a few lines on the bottom of the page or in a box or sidebar, the illustration taking the majority of the space. But in every case, and most important, the illustration was tied to the text. On July 29, for example, the *Post* printed a piece called "Earning and Education: How Much Money Should the Student Have?" It was illustrated with two pictures: one of a man and one of a woman, each carrying a book in one hand and a bag of money in the other.

All of these experiments, however, took place not on a cover but on the first page of each issue, for, as the page numbering reveals, a cover still did not exist as a separate entity. At this time, the *Post* used continuous page numbering through a whole "volume," including the first page. And at this time, the magazine was still published in its old oversized format, approximately 11 by 17 inches.

All that changed on September 30, 1899. That issue appeared in a new size, the now long-familiar 11 by 14 inches, and at 30 pages, it was the largest issue to date. For the first time, a separate cover, in color, graced the *Post*. The historic first cover illustration was a painting by George Gibbs, who produced scores of the magazine's early covers. For this issue, however, he painted a sea scene, as an illustration for the first installment of a long series by Cyrus Townsend Brady, called "For the Freedom of the Sea."

The *Post* had waited more than two years for its first cover. The September 30 issue was not only the first *Post* cover, it marked the beginning of *Post* advertising on a grand scale. Along with a front cover came three more pages, unnumbered, all of them available to advertisers. The two-color red-and-black format used on the front carried over to the back, and Quaker Oats bought the whole page, something of a rarity at that time. The two inside covers, in black and white, were sold in pieces, four in the front, and three in the back. The new cover was costly; advertising helped to recoup the expense.

Still, the appearance of a real cover for September 30 did not mean that Lorimer had found a formula. For the rest of the year the magazine alternated between two-color covers with a full-page painting and those in black and white with both text and ornamentation. The more expensive color covers were reserved for special holiday issues. Thanksgiving was the occasion for a Pilgrim couple (November 25), and the Christmas number presented the graceful work of Henry Hutt, who painted a man and woman in a carriage, engaged in their Christmas shopping (December 23).

But during the fall of 1899, black-and-white covers predominated, and often carried attractive illustrations. On October 28, for "The College Man's Issue," Frank X.

Leyendecker, brother of the more famous J. C. (Joseph Christian), rendered two college men, one in a football uniform, the other in a robe and mortarboard. And in this early period, some black-and-white covers featured photographs. On October 21, a new poem by Edwin Markham, made famous by "The Man with the Hoe," began on the cover alongside a photograph of the poet in the woods.

Although photographs would virtually disappear from the cover for the rest of Lorimer's editorship, reappearing only when Wesley Stout took over in 1937, these earliest covers frequently showed experiments with photography. To decorate Thomas B. Reed's "Paris and French Justice," the October 7 cover presented a drawing of the figure of Justice above a framed photograph of Paris. And for the last issue of 1899, on December 30, the cover was divided in two. On the top was a photograph of New York City below a drawing of New York in the seventeenth century. The *Saturday Evening Post* was ushering in the new century with a piece by Carter H. Harrison, mayor of Chicago, called "The Twentieth Century City."

In these last months of the nineteenth century, the *Post* tried out not only new cover formats but also new uses for the cover. Of the possible uses two were exploited most often, but one was soon discontinued while the other became a *Post* institution.

Lorimer discarded the cover illustration that supported an article or piece of fiction; in its place, the magazine simply advertised the authors and/or the titles of one or more important pieces in the issue. It was perhaps the work of Harrison Fisher that first broke away from illustrating a story or article to presenting images that were simply appealing in their own right.

Although Fisher's earliest cover work for the *Post* had been restricted to story illustration, for April 14, 1900, he painted a romantic picture that showed an elegant young couple on a porch taking tea together. On August 25, he repeated that romantic theme, setting a couple on the porch of a summer hotel. Once again, late in the year, he painted another such couple, in a horse-drawn sleigh (November 10). While color covers were still a rarity, appearing only about once a month, Fisher's elegant men and women were printed in color.

What became a *Post* institution was the holiday cover: for decades the magazine signaled New Year's Day, Valentine's Day, Easter, the Fourth of July, Thanksgiving, and Christmas with thematic illustrations. These holiday covers belonged to the magazine's most famous and best-loved illustrators, especially Rockwell and Leyendecker.

But no illustrator, whatever his fame, had control over a cover of the *Post*. Like everything else in the magazine, the cover belonged to Lorimer. He would review a set of potential covers rapidly, dismissing most with a cursory glance and a terse "Out." As Norman Rockwell described it in his autobiography, Lorimer's comments were limited to "Bad" and "Good," the "Good" illustrations ratified by a scrawled "OKGHL" on the side."*

The principal function the covers would come to serve was the representation of America or, more precisely, of America's ideas about itself. Such representation did not take the form of realistic images of all the varieties of American experience; rather, it expressed images that stirred common

*Norman Rockwell, as told to Thomas Rockwell, *Norman Rockwell: My Adventures as an Illustrator* (Indianapolis: Curtis Publishing Company, 1979). For histories of the *Saturday Evening Post* under Lorimer's editorship see John Tebbel, *George Horace Lorimer and "The Saturday Evening Post"* (Garden City, N.Y.: Doubleday, 1948), and Jan Cohn, *Creating America: George Horace Lorimer and the "Saturday Evening Post"* (Pittsburgh: University of Pittsburgh Press, 1989).

feelings and appealed to shared ideals, whether these were portraits of lovely women, or whimsical pictures of little girls, or comic drawings of old folks and little boys.

Finally, the covers of the *Post* became more than their subjects and more than the artists who rendered them. The *Saturday Evening Post*'s covers became what might be called the most visible token of the magazine. Unmistakable, the covers of the *Post* became a weekly symbol of its presence, its longevity, its vast circulation. No clearer index of the self-assurance of the magazine can be seen than the way in which the cover art was allowed to intrude on the title itself. In the earliest years, the title was set off on the top of the page, surrounded by a heavy line. Illustration, with or without accompanying text, was clearly separated from the name of the magazine.

The heavy border that set off the name of the *Post* was abandoned when the now-familiar typeface for the title was adopted in 1904. The title and the cover art were separated either by a double line between them or, occasionally, by a border around the art. What is striking is the way in which the cover art was gradually allowed to block out parts of the title. As early as 1903, Harrison Fisher painted the head of a woman that covered part of the familiar statement of "Five Cents the Copy." Over time, some art blocked out part of the magazine title itself until, by the late 1920s and early 1930s, this device had become commonplace. Eventually the cover itself, particularly when it was illustrated by an artist as familiar as Rockwell or Leyendecker, rather than the name of the magazine, became the sign of the *Post*.

THE SATURDAY EVENING POST

An Illustrated Weekly Magazine
Founded Aº Dº 1728 by Benj. Franklin

Volume 172. No. 27   Philadelphia, December 30, 1899   5 Cents the Copy; $2.50 the Year

The Twentieth Century City
By Carter H. Harrison, Mayor of Chicago

THE BEGINNINGS OF OUR GREATEST AMERICAN CITY—NEW YORK IN THE 17TH CENTURY

Winfield S. Lukens
DECEMBER 30, 1899

CHAPTER I

THE FIRST DECADE

In the December 30, 1899, issue, the *Saturday Evening Post* welcomed the new year with a two-page advertisement for itself. "Post's Plans for 1900" laid out policies and promises, claimed a national audience, and stated that the *Post*, edited for the "average American," would "become the indispensable magazine."

This was a bold assertion for a magazine whose weekly circulation that month had averaged only 108,000 and whose losses since Curtis's purchase in mid-1897 now reached nearly a million dollars. Nevertheless, the promise would be fulfilled within the decade.

The *Post*'s financial picture brightened immediately. Losses gave way to profits as early as October 1900, when for the first time monthly receipts exceeded payments. Advertising steadily increased, and by late in the decade as much as 60 percent of an issue was filled with advertising. Circulation also continued to rise, until the December 12, 1908, issue could announce on the cover that circulation exceeded 1,000,000 a week. And throughout the decade, both fiction and nonfiction made good Lorimer's December 30, 1899, promise that he would "secure the greatest living writers."

Post covers, too, reflected the success story of the magazine. The year 1899 had closed with two black-and-white representations of New York. By contrast, three of the four December issues in 1909, beautifully produced in red and black, worked a set of holiday themes. On December 4, J. C. Leyendecker portrayed a family man on his way home, laden with Christmas presents. On December 18, Leyendecker's work appeared again (top left, page 4): a seasonal contrast of rich and poor, old and young, this cover featured a portly rich man in a fur-lined coat searching his coin purse for money to buy a paper from a small boy, who wears only a jacket against the weather and stands on a grating for warmth. The cover for December 25 featured the work of Sarah Stilwell-Weber, whose specialty was small children. For this cover she painted a small boy surrounded with toys. The same cover noted proudly a circulation of 1,250,000.

Four artists, each of whom painted more than forty covers in these years, dominated the *Post*'s covers during the first decade of the century. These artists were George Gibbs and Guernsey Moore, who did most of their work in the first half of the decade, and Harrison Fisher and J. C. Leyendecker, whose contributions increased over the later years.

Both Gibbs and Moore were compe-

tent illustrators, and both could depict romanticized historical scenes and subjects that were much to Lorimer's taste at this time. Lorimer believed that one important aim for the *Post* was to create a sense of nationalism strong enough to override America's regional differences. Thus, just as nonfiction frequently turned to American history for subject matter, these covers mined the same material to create the visual representations of heroic and sentimental episodes.

Sometimes these historical covers simply portrayed a particular American hero, as in Gibbs's February 15, 1902, depiction of George Washington surrounded by other Revolutionary leaders, or Moore's January 20, 1906, portrait of Ben Franklin with his famous kite, painted in celebration of the bicentennial anniversary of Franklin's birth (bottom, page 9). More often, the covers evoked the past in a more general way. Gibbs drew a Confederate officer to emphasize that we were again one nation (February 6, 1904; top right, page 10), and Moore acknowledged Thanksgiving with a woman in colonial dress trimming a pie (November 18, 1905; bottom left, page 4). J. J. Gould and Moore collaborated on the March 7, 1903, cover (top, page 9), another that emphasized the *Post*'s descent from Franklin: they painted Franklin as a young man at his printing press, with the caption "Franklin's First Number."

It was not only in representing historical subjects that the covers reflected Lorimer's editorial ideas for the *Post*. The editor's principal goal was to have his magazine reflect the interests of the "average American," and those interests, Lorimer believed, were overwhelmingly business interests. Thus, business and the businessman became prime subjects. Lorimer worked hard to seek out, and to encourage the writ-

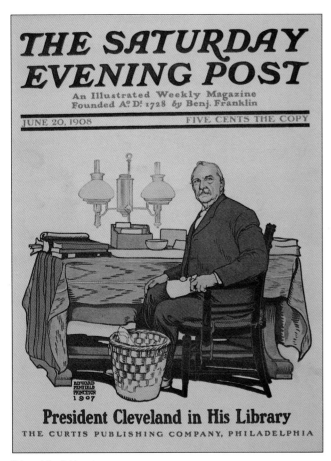

Edward Penfield
JUNE 20, 1908

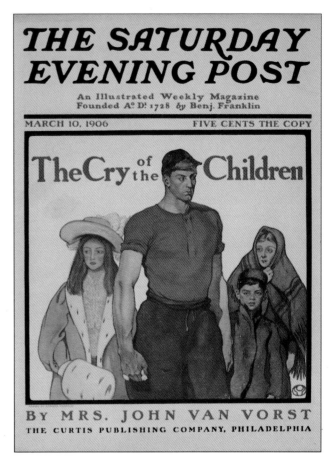

Edward Penfield
MARCH 10, 1906

J. C. Leyendecker
OCTOBER 31, 1908

J. C. Leyendecker
MARCH 6, 1909

J. C. Leyendecker
DECEMBER 18, 1909

J. C. Leyendecker
DECEMBER 3, 1904

Guernsey Moore
NOVEMBER 18, 1905

Harrison Fisher
DECEMBER 12, 1908

ing of, business fiction; the *Post* serialized the most important examples of such fiction during this period, including Harold Frederic's *The Market-Place*, Frank Norris's *The Pit*, and Robert Herrick's *The Memoirs of an American Citizen* (announced with a cover illustration showing a young man gazing at Chicago, a scene filled with trains, barges, chimneys, and smoke). But the *Post*'s most successful piece of business fiction was written by Lorimer himself. Serialized anonymously in 1901–2, *Letters from a Self-Made Merchant to His Son* was an instant success and, republished in book form, became a best-seller in America and abroad.

If it was difficult to find first-rate fiction on the subject of business, it was even harder to elicit first-rate cover art on this topic. Carefully, the *Post* defined business broadly enough; articles and back-of-the-book features extended the meaning of "businessmen" to include artists, writers, and even ministers. Still, the fundamental concepts connected to business were much narrower; ideas associated with factories and offices left little room for the creative play of the illustrator's imagination. Still, an occasional cover demonstrated that an artist was trying to present the business idea more or less straight. For the October 10, 1903, issue James Preston did a picture of Wall Street itself, and three years later F. R. Gruger painted a stock market scene (October 13, 1906).

But for the purposes of graphic art, the visual associations with business needed to be much extended. J. J. Gould had some early successes looking at the laboring side of business. For the June 28, 1902, cover he presented a factory worker with mills in the background. Over the next couple of years he painted a lumberjack (April 4, 1903) and a railroad worker (January 16, 1904). Gould was particularly successful in developing images that reflected the rise of cities in relation to business, and the growing distance between rural and urban America. For September 19, 1903, he depicted a plowman and his horse with city smokestacks in the distance. Edward Penfield replicated this theme with a team of draft horses hauling a wagon carrying a large machine (May 14, 1904). Another, and very unusual, cover by Penfield returned to the idea of labor, in this case illustrating a family of immigrant laborers for the March 10, 1906, issue (top right, page 3).

Among business subjects, railroads were a consuming editorial interest in the *Post* and a viable subject for painters. One of Frank B. Masters's few covers for the magazine showed a railroad surveyor for October 1, 1904, and for the next week's cover Emlen McConnell painted a railroad engineer carrying an oil can. Masters later painted a more dramatic cover, showing a locomotive steaming through a blizzard (March 3, 1906; bottom right, page 10).

When Teddy Roosevelt began his trust-busting, the *Post* went along, with a small number of covers attacking business excesses. These had something of the flavor of political cartoons. The May 4, 1907, cover showed a Harry B. Lachman image of a pirate with a bag of booty labeled "R. R. Steel." That fall, Leyendecker painted a gross plutocrat, Get Rich Quick Wallingford (October 5, 1907). As it turned out, this was not a road the magazine would be tempted to follow again; no doubt the astringency of such art defeated the primary intention of the *Post* cover, which aimed at a more general appeal.

Two other important themes for the *Post* were much more amenable to artistic interpretation than was business. These were the complementary themes of nature and the West, which depended upon the notion that the West was where real nature could be found. Teddy Roosevelt had popularized the West for many Americans, including Lorimer, who became an annual tourist to the new national parks. But the West had another appeal as well, and that appeal came through fiction. The *Post* printed western stories from the beginning, from the work of Bret Harte on through decades of new writers. Like these stories, many western covers on the *Post* featured stereotypical western characters—cowboys, gunslingers, miners.

Several artists contributed western covers, among them the well-known N. C. Wyeth. Wyeth's cover work for the *Post* included a cowboy on a bucking bronco (February 21, 1903); Oliver Kemp painted a pair of French-Canadian trappers portaging their canoe (June 19, 1909; top left, page 10). George Gibbs tried his hand at the western mode too. For June 14, 1902, he painted a gold miner with his pickax and gun (top right, page 11).

Most of the *Post*'s nature covers were painted by Paul Bransom and Charles Livingston Bull, the latter being one of the period's premier nature artists. Bull's work began appearing in 1903, with a depiction of a sled dog (June 20, 1903; bottom left, page 11); later that year he drew a circus tiger and a hoop. Bransom began cover work for the *Post* in 1907, with three hounds in full chase (February 16, 1907), and, a few weeks later, an owl flying across a full moon (March 2, 1907; center left, page 11).

The West and nature merged in some covers. Emlen McConnell's cover for May 21, 1904, shows a westerner staring out across his land. For September 22, 1906, Edward Penfield painted one cowboy looking across an expanse of dry land at two other cowboys, who watch over a small herd of cattle (bottom left, page 10). Later that year, Wyeth simply silhouetted the head of a cowboy against the setting sun (November 30, 1907).

Some western covers took the form of genre paintings, particularly those of Oliver Kemp. For May 2, 1908, he painted a lone western man cooking his dinner over a campfire. The next year, he represented the same idea of loneliness and self-sufficiency in a picture of an Indian paddling his canoe through a barren landscape.

Many of the covers of the *Post* in this first decade reflected the interests of the editor, and thus complemented in a general way the ideas presented in the articles and stories published in the magazine. But historical scenes, business subjects, nature, and the West did not, either separately or in the aggregate, make up the majority of *Saturday Evening Post* covers. The major theme for the cover art for the *Post* had virtually nothing to do with the editorial content. Dominating the covers was a portrait of a woman, one version or another of the American girl. Pictures of females, adult or child, alone or as part of a couple, made up fully half of the covers of the *Post* in these years.

A number of *Post* artists concentrated their efforts on portraits of women, but the most important work in this early period was made up of the elegant paintings of Harrison Fisher. Fisher, along with Henry Hutt, frequently painted covers that simply presented a lovely woman. Fisher also painted couples in scenes that suggested decorous romance, on a porch or drinking tea. Sometimes there was a seasonal theme: the December 12, 1908, cover that announced a 1,000,000 circulation had a Fisher portrait of a handsome woman hanging a sprig of mistletoe (bottom right, page 4). Occasionally a prop, perhaps a tennis racquet or a

J. C. Leyendecker
DECEMBER 29, 1906

J. C. Leyendecker
DECEMBER 28, 1907

J. C. Leyendecker
DECEMBER 26, 1908

J. C. Leyendecker
NOVEMBER 13, 1909

football pennant, implied a narrative, but the essential subject remained the woman herself.

The most important, and the most versatile, of *Post* cover artists in this decade was J. C. Leyendecker. Leyendecker could turn his hand to any subject, from business to history to women and more. Over time, he would paint more than three hundred covers for the *Post* and, until the advent of Norman Rockwell, he was surely the artist most closely associated with the cover of the magazine.

Leyendecker's style was strong and angular. His square-jawed, clear-eyed men all more or less resembled the Arrow Collar Man he invented, but his style was fluid enough to encompass paintings of women and children. Moreover, he was capable of shifting his tone; his covers could be serious or romantic or satiric or comic. He could strike the imperial note, as in his March 6, 1909, cover for the Taft inauguration, showing a huge President Taft before an equally huge flag-draped chair (bottom right, page 3). He could be sentimental, as on the March 23, 1907, cover, with a little girl gathering Easter eggs. And when he had the occasion, he could dress his paintings up with richly decorated ornaments and finely articulated textures; for December 3, 1904, he painted a woman in medieval dress carrying a plum pudding (top right, page 4).

But in these years Leyendecker became best known for his holiday covers. Beginning in 1899, Lorimer had marked Thanksgiving and Christmas with special covers, and by the middle of the decade, New Year's and Easter boasted seasonal paintings as well. By 1908, Valentine's Day had been added, as had the Fourth of July. Leyendecker painted almost all these holiday covers. And the most important of them were the ones for the New Year, because for that occasion Leyendecker invented his New Year baby.

The New Year baby first appeared on the December 29, 1906, issue, with the legend "1907" painted in black (top left, page 7). The star of the illustration was the baby, a girl in this first incarnation. Complete with a bow in her hair, she sits with a large book and a pencil, filling in her resolutions. A year later, the baby, now a boy, has returned with a stork (December 28, 1907; top right, page 7). The New Year baby would appear for decades, making Leyendecker's and the *Post*'s comment on the national mood or the international situation. The baby made its last appearance during World War II; on January 2, 1942, the Leyendecker baby appeared naked but helmeted, as he vigorously set about destroying a German swastika.

At first, the baby was not restricted to the New Year but made other casual appearances. Dressed in an apron and chef's cap, he is seen sharpening his carv-ing knife for Thanksgiving (November 13, 1909; bottom right, page 7). But for the most part, Leyendecker tried out other ideas for other holidays: for the Fourth of July, 1908, a nineteenth-century orator; for Thanksgiving, 1907, a pilgrim stalking a turkey (November 23); for Easter, 1905, a bonneted woman in church (April 22); and for Christmas, 1908, a little girl standing under the mistletoe near a shy little boy holding a dance card (December 26; bottom left, page 7).

The closing years of the decade saw two more new ideas realized on the covers of the magazine. In 1908, the *Post* began experimenting with current events and national personalities for cover illustrations. For June 20, 1908, Edward Penfield sketched a serious, dignified portrait of Grover Cleveland, with the caption "President Cleveland in His Library" (top left, page 3). That same year, Election Day was marked with a Leyendecker cover depicting a newsboy holding pictures of Taft and Bryan, with the single-word caption "Which?" (bottom left, page 3).

The second new idea was the celebration of sports, specifically of modern mass-audience sports. These covers featured action, implying in a single moment the progress of the entire game, with all its excitement and uncertainty. Frank X. Leyendecker (J. C.'s brother) drew two hockey players in action for the January 11, 1908, cover. In the spring of 1909, the versatile J. C. Leyendecker tried his hand at sports, with a catcher, mask down and mitt up, ready for the ball (May 15).

To the contemporary eye, *Post* covers for the first decade of the century may seem understated and restrained, but they were, in fact, very modern, up to date. The two-color, red-and-black, production of the art did not yet have to compete with the bolder, brighter statements of four-color covers. More important, the quality of the illustrations was very high, and it continued to improve. By the end of the decade, the covers of the *Post* were, like the magazine itself, fully incorporated into American mass culture. In the quality of the work and in the range of subjects, the covers had indeed become a reflection of America's ideas about itself.

J. J. Gould & Guernsey Moore
MARCH 7, 1903

Guernsey Moore
JANUARY 20, 1906

Oliver Kemp
JUNE 19, 1909

George Gibbs
FEBRUARY 6, 1904

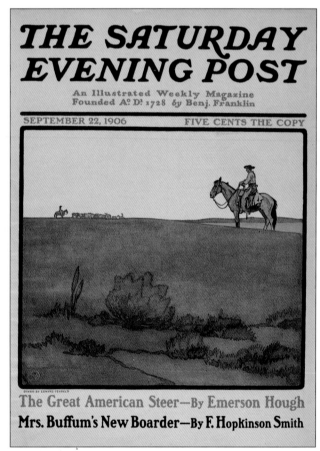

Edward Penfield
SEPTEMBER 22, 1906

Frank B. Masters
MARCH 3, 1906

Charles Livingston Bull
JULY 3, 1909

Paul Bransom
MARCH 2, 1907

Charles Livingston Bull
JUNE 20, 1903

George Gibbs
JUNE 14, 1902

Oliver Kemp
OCTOBER 2, 1909

Harrison Fisher
JANUARY 6, 1900

J. J. Gould & George Gibbs
JANUARY 13, 1900

Gustave Verbeek
JANUARY 20, 1900

George Gibbs
JANUARY 27, 1900

Harry C. Edwards
FEBRUARY 3, 1900

C. Hay
FEBRUARY 10, 1900

Karl Kleinschmidt
FEBRUARY 17, 1900

George Gibbs
MARCH 3, 1900

Gustave Verbeek
MARCH 10, 1900

George Gibbs
MARCH 17, 1900

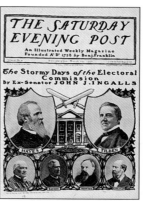

Sarony & Bell
MARCH 24, 1900

George Gibbs
MARCH 31, 1900

Artist unknown
APRIL 7, 1900

Harrison Fisher
APRIL 14, 1900

George Gibbs
APRIL 21, 1900

Harrison Fisher
APRIL 28, 1900

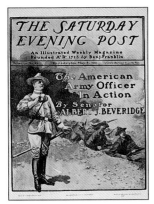

Martin Justice
MAY 5, 1900

Henry Hutt
MAY 12, 1900

George Gibbs
MAY 19, 1900

Frank X. Leyendecker
MAY 26, 1900

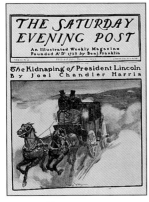

George Gibbs
JUNE 2, 1900

J. Clay
JUNE 9, 1900

Harrison Fisher
JUNE 16, 1900

Artist unknown
JUNE 23, 1900

Guernsey Moore
JUNE 30, 1900

Frank X. Leyendecker
JULY 7, 1900

Artist unknown
JULY 14, 1900

George Gibbs
JULY 28, 1900

J. Clay
AUGUST 4, 1900

George Gibbs
AUGUST 11, 1900

Mills Thompson
AUGUST 18, 1900

Harrison Fisher
AUGUST 25, 1900

George Gibbs
SEPTEMBER 1, 1900

George Gibbs
SEPTEMBER 8, 1900

Artist unknown
SEPTEMBER 29, 1900

Mills Thompson
OCTOBER 6, 1900

Mills Thompson
OCTOBER 13, 1900

Henry Hutt & George Gibbs
OCTOBER 20, 1900

Artist unknown
OCTOBER 27, 1900

Guernsey Moore
NOVEMBER 3, 1900

Harrison Fisher
NOVEMBER 10, 1900

Artist unknown
NOVEMBER 17, 1900

George Gibbs
NOVEMBER 24, 1900

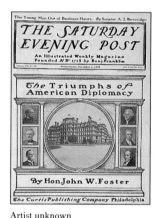

Artist unknown
DECEMBER 1, 1900

George Gibbs
DECEMBER 8, 1900

Artist unknown
DECEMBER 15, 1900

Artist unknown
DECEMBER 22, 1900

George Gibbs
DECEMBER 29, 1900

George Gibbs
JANUARY 5, 1901

Artist unknown
JANUARY 12, 1901

George Gibbs
JANUARY 26, 1901

George Gibbs
FEBRUARY 2, 1901

J. J. Gould & Guernsey Moore
MARCH 2, 1901

Purdy
MARCH 16, 1901

Frank X. Leyendecker
MARCH 23, 1901

Guernsey Moore
APRIL 6, 1901

Harry C. Edwards
APRIL 13, 1901

George Gibbs
APRIL 20, 1901

George Gibbs
APRIL 27, 1901

Guernsey Moore
MAY 4, 1901

Harrison Fisher
MAY 11, 1901

Artist unknown
MAY 18, 1901

Guernsey Moore
MAY 25, 1901

Guernsey Moore
JUNE 1, 1901

Artist unknown
JUNE 8, 1901

Artist unknown
JUNE 15, 1901

Frank X. Leyendecker
JUNE 22, 1901

George Gibbs
JUNE 29, 1901

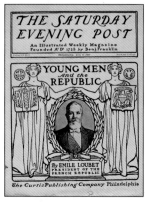

Guernsey Moore
JULY 6, 1901

George Gibbs
JULY 13, 1901

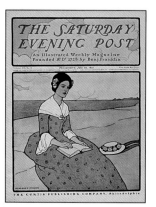

Guernsey Moore
JULY 20, 1901

Artist unknown
JULY 27, 1901

Guernsey Moore
AUGUST 3, 1901

J. J. Gould
AUGUST 10, 1901

Artist unknown
AUGUST 17, 1901

Harrison Fisher
AUGUST 24, 1901

Artist unknown
AUGUST 31, 1901

Artist unknown
SEPTEMBER 7, 1901

J. J. Gould
SEPTEMBER 14, 1901

Guernsey Moore
SEPTEMBER 21, 1901

Guernsey Moore
SEPTEMBER 28, 1901

Photograph
OCTOBER 5, 1901

George Gibbs
OCTOBER 12, 1901

Artist unknown
OCTOBER 19, 1901

Guernsey Moore
OCTOBER 26, 1901

Artist unknown
NOVEMBER 2, 1901

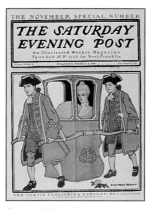

Guernsey Moore
NOVEMBER 9, 1901

George Gibbs
NOVEMBER 16, 1901

Guernsey Moore
NOVEMBER 23, 1901

Guernsey Moore
NOVEMBER 30, 1901

Frederic Remington
DECEMBER 14, 1901

Guernsey Moore
DECEMBER 21, 1901

George Gibbs
DECEMBER 28, 1901

J. J. Gould & Guernsey Moore
JANUARY 4, 1902

Guernsey Moore
JANUARY 11, 1902

George Gibbs
JANUARY 18, 1902

George Gibbs
JANUARY 25, 1902

Guernsey Moore
FEBRUARY 1, 1902

Guernsey Moore
FEBRUARY 8, 1902

George Gibbs
FEBRUARY 15, 1902

Harrison Fisher
FEBRUARY 22, 1902

Harrison Fisher
MARCH 1, 1902

Guernsey Moore
MARCH 8, 1902

George Gibbs
MARCH 15, 1902

Guernsey Moore
MARCH 22, 1902

George Gibbs
MARCH 29, 1902

Guernsey Moore
APRIL 5, 1902

George Gibbs
APRIL 12, 1902

Harry C. Edwards
APRIL 19, 1902

George Gibbs
APRIL 26, 1902

Artist unknown
MAY 3, 1902

Harrison Fisher
MAY 10, 1902

Guernsey Moore
MAY 17, 1902

Guernsey Moore
MAY 24, 1902

Frank X. Leyendecker
MAY 31, 1902

Guernsey Moore
JUNE 7, 1902

Harrison Fisher
JUNE 21, 1902

J. J. Gould
JUNE 28, 1902

Walter Whitehead
JULY 5, 1902

Artist unknown
JULY 12, 1902

J. J. Gould
JULY 26, 1902

George Gibbs
AUGUST 2, 1902

Artist unknown
AUGUST 9, 1902

Harrison Fisher
AUGUST 16, 1902

Pete Fountain
AUGUST 23, 1902

Pete Fountain
AUGUST 30, 1902

George Gibbs
SEPTEMBER 6, 1902

Walter Whitehead
SEPTEMBER 13, 1902

19

Will Grefe
SEPTEMBER 20, 1902

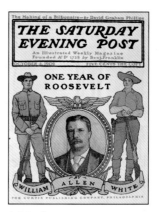

Henry Hutt
SEPTEMBER 27, 1902

Artist unknown
OCTOBER 4, 1902

Pete Fountain
OCTOBER 11, 1902

Artist unknown
OCTOBER 18, 1902

J. J. Gould
OCTOBER 25, 1902

Harrison Fisher
NOVEMBER 1, 1902

George Gibbs
NOVEMBER 8, 1902

Charles Livingston Bull
NOVEMBER 15, 1902

J. J. Gould & Guernsey Moore
NOVEMBER 22, 1902

Pete Fountain
NOVEMBER 29, 1902

J. J. Gould & Guernsey Moore
DECEMBER 6, 1902

George Gibbs
DECEMBER 13, 1902

Henry Hutt
DECEMBER 20, 1902

Henry Hutt
DECEMBER 27, 1902

Harrison Fisher
JANUARY 10, 1903

Pete Fountain
JANUARY 17, 1903

Harrison Fisher
JANUARY 24, 1903

Artist unknown
JANUARY 31, 1903

J. C. Leyendecker
FEBRUARY 7, 1903

J. J. Gould
FEBRUARY 14, 1903

Harrison Fisher
FEBRUARY 28, 1903

Harrison Fisher
MARCH 14, 1903

Pete Fountain
MARCH 21, 1903

George Gibbs
MARCH 28, 1903

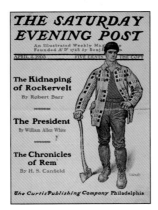

J. J. Gould
APRIL 4, 1903

Henry Hutt
APRIL 11, 1903

Harrison Fisher
APRIL 18, 1903

Harrison Fisher
APRIL 25, 1903

Ethel Franklin Betts
MAY 2, 1903

George Gibbs
MAY 9, 1903

J. C. Leyendecker
MAY 16, 1903

Harrison Fisher
MAY 23, 1903

S. D. Runyon
MAY 30, 1903

J. J. Gould
JUNE 6, 1903

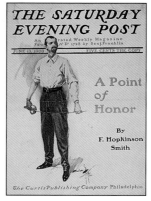

Harrison Fisher
JUNE 13, 1903

J. J. Gould & Guernsey Moore
JUNE 27, 1903

J. J. Gould
JULY 4, 1903

Artist unknown
JULY 11, 1903

S. D. Runyon
JULY 18, 1903

Frances Vaux Wilson
JULY 25, 1903

Guernsey Moore
AUGUST 1, 1903

Edward Penfield
AUGUST 8, 1903

J. J. Gould & Guernsey Moore
AUGUST 15, 1903

Edward Penfield
AUGUST 22, 1903

Emlen McConnell
AUGUST 29, 1903

Edward Penfield
SEPTEMBER 5, 1903

Guernsey Moore
SEPTEMBER 12, 1903

J. J. Gould
SEPTEMBER 19, 1903

Frank X. Leyendecker
SEPTEMBER 26, 1903

F. R. Gruger
OCTOBER 3, 1903

James Preston
OCTOBER 10, 1903

Charles Livingston Bull
OCTOBER 17, 1903

Guernsey Moore
OCTOBER 24, 1903

Edward Penfield
OCTOBER 31, 1903

Guernsey Moore
NOVEMBER 7, 1903

Harrison Fisher
NOVEMBER 14, 1903

Guernsey Moore
NOVEMBER 21, 1903

George Gibbs
NOVEMBER 28, 1903

Clarence Underwood
DECEMBER 5, 1903

Frank Walter Taylor
DECEMBER 12, 1903

Guernsey Moore
DECEMBER 19, 1903

Harrison Fisher
DECEMBER 26, 1903

Ethel Franklin Betts
JANUARY 2, 1904

Heinrich Pfeifer
JANUARY 9, 1904

J. J. Gould
JANUARY 16, 1904

Artist unknown
JANUARY 23, 1904

Guernsey Moore
JANUARY 30, 1904

Ethel Franklin Betts
FEBRUARY 13, 1904

J. J. Gould
FEBRUARY 20, 1904

Edward Penfield
FEBRUARY 27, 1904

Will Grefe
MARCH 5, 1904

J. J. Gould
MARCH 12, 1904

Walter Whitehead
MARCH 19, 1904

Karl Anderson
MARCH 26, 1904

Guernsey Moore
APRIL 2, 1904

Guernsey Moore
APRIL 9, 1904

James Preston
APRIL 16, 1904

Guernsey Moore
APRIL 23, 1904

Karl Anderson
APRIL 30, 1904

24

J. J. Gould
MAY 7, 1904

Edward Penfield
MAY 14, 1904

Emlen McConnell
MAY 21, 1904

Henry Hutt
MAY 28, 1904

James Preston
JUNE 4, 1904

J. C. Leyendecker
JUNE 11, 1904

J. J. Gould
JUNE 18, 1904

Henry Hutt
JUNE 25, 1904

J. J. Gould
JULY 2, 1904

J. C. Leyendecker
JULY 9, 1904

Henry Hutt
JULY 16, 1904

Harrison Fisher
JULY 23, 1904

Emlen McConnell
JULY 30, 1904

Will Grefe
AUGUST 6, 1904

J. J. Gould
AUGUST 13, 1904

Henry Hutt
AUGUST 20, 1904

25

James Preston
AUGUST 27, 1904

Henry Hutt
SEPTEMBER 3, 1904

James Preston
SEPTEMBER 10, 1904

Henry Hutt
SEPTEMBER 17, 1904

Frank B. Masters
OCTOBER 1, 1904

Emlen McConnell
OCTOBER 8, 1904

Walter H. Everett
OCTOBER 15, 1904

J. C. Leyendecker
OCTOBER 22, 1904

Anne Estelle Rice
OCTOBER 29, 1904

Harrison Fisher
NOVEMBER 5, 1904

Karl Anderson
NOVEMBER 12, 1904

Guernsey Moore
NOVEMBER 19, 1904

James Preston
NOVEMBER 26, 1904

Karl Anderson
DECEMBER 10, 1904

Emlen McConnell
DECEMBER 17, 1904

Guernsey Moore
DECEMBER 24, 1904

Sarah Stilwell-Weber
DECEMBER 31, 1904

Harrison Fisher
JANUARY 7, 1905

J. L. S. Williams
JANUARY 14, 1905

Karl Anderson
JANUARY 21, 1905

266 Guernsey Moore
JANUARY 28, 1905

Karl Anderson
FEBRUARY 4, 1905

Guernsey Moore
FEBRUARY 11, 1905

J. J. Gould
FEBRUARY 18, 1905

Clarence Underwood
FEBRUARY 25, 1905

Edward Penfield
MARCH 4, 1905

Anne Estelle Rice
MARCH 11, 1905

J. C. Leyendecker
MARCH 18, 1905

Frank X. Leyendecker
MARCH 25, 1905

Frank B. Masters
APRIL 1, 1905

Charles Livingston Bull
APRIL 8, 1905

Guernsey Moore
APRIL 15, 1905

J. C. Leyendecker
APRIL 22, 1905

James Preston
APRIL 29, 1905

Guernsey Moore
MAY 6, 1905

Guernsey Moore
MAY 13, 1905

N. C. Wyeth
MAY 20, 1905

Grace Evans
MAY 27, 1905

J. C. Leyendecker
JUNE 3, 1905

Carl A. Strehlau
JUNE 10, 1905

Edward Penfield
JUNE 17, 1905

Artist unknown
JUNE 24, 1905

Walter H. Everett
JULY 1, 1905

Guernsey Moore
JULY 8, 1905

George Gibbs
JULY 15, 1905

Henrietta Adams
JULY 22, 1905

Anne Estelle Rice
JULY 29, 1905

Guernsey Moore
AUGUST 5, 1905

Guernsey Moore
AUGUST 12, 1905

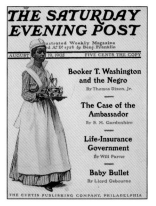

Artist unknown
AUGUST 19, 1905

Artist unknown
AUGUST 26, 1905

H. Lyman Sayen
SEPTEMBER 2, 1905

Charles Livingston Bull
SEPTEMBER 9, 1905

Jay Vaughn McFall
SEPTEMBER 16, 1905

Will Grefe
SEPTEMBER 23, 1905

Will Grefe
SEPTEMBER 30, 1905

Walter H. Everett
OCTOBER 7, 1905

Philip R. Goodwin
OCTOBER 14, 1905

Edward Penfield
OCTOBER 21, 1905

Guernsey Moore
OCTOBER 28, 1905

Gordon Grant
NOVEMBER 4, 1905

Walter Appleton Clark
NOVEMBER 11, 1905

Guernsey Moore
NOVEMBER 25, 1905

J. C. Leyendecker
DECEMBER 2, 1905

Artist unknown,
DECEMBER 9, 1905

Will Grefe
DECEMBER 16, 1905

Guernsey Moore
DECEMBER 23, 1905

Henry Hutt
DECEMBER 30, 1905

H. Irving Marlatt
JANUARY 6, 1906

Karl Anderson
JANUARY 13, 1906

J. C. Leyendecker
JANUARY 27, 1906

Philip R. Goodwin
FEBRUARY 3, 1906

Henry Hutt
FEBRUARY 10, 1906

J. J. Gould
FEBRUARY 17, 1906

Gordon Grant
FEBRUARY 24, 1906

Henry Hutt
MARCH 17, 1906

Allan Gilbert
MARCH 24, 1906

Guernsey Moore
MARCH 31, 1906

J. C. Leyendecker
APRIL 7, 1906

Karl Anderson
APRIL 14, 1906

Remington Schuyler
APRIL 21, 1906

Albert Sterner
APRIL 28, 1906

Fanny Young Cory
MAY 5, 1906

Sarah Stilwell-Weber
MAY 12, 1906

Edward Penfield
MAY 19, 1906

Edward Penfield
MAY 26, 1906

J. C. Leyendecker
JUNE 2, 1906

Philip R. Goodwin
JUNE 9, 1906

Henry Hutt
JUNE 16, 1906

Will Grefe
JUNE 23, 1906

Guernsey Moore
JUNE 30, 1906

Guernsey Moore
JULY 7, 1906

H. Lyman Sayen
JULY 14, 1906

Guernsey Moore
JULY 21, 1906

P. V. E. Ivory
JULY 28, 1906

Henry Hutt
AUGUST 4, 1906

Harry B. Lachman
AUGUST 11, 1906

F. Rogers
AUGUST 18, 1906

F. Rogers
AUGUST 25, 1906

Hermann C. Wall
SEPTEMBER 1, 1906

Will Grefe
SEPTEMBER 8, 1906

Karl Anderson
SEPTEMBER 15, 1906

Katharine Richardson Wireman
SEPTEMBER 29, 1906

Karl Anderson
OCTOBER 6, 1906

F. R. Gruger
OCTOBER 13, 1906

Charles Livingston Bull
OCTOBER 20, 1906

Edward Penfield
OCTOBER 27, 1906

Artist unknown
NOVEMBER 3, 1906

F. R. Gruger
NOVEMBER 10, 1906

Artist unknown
NOVEMBER 17, 1906

Edward Penfield
NOVEMBER 24, 1906

J. C. Leyendecker
DECEMBER 1, 1906

Albert Beck Wenzell
DECEMBER 8, 1906

George Brehm
DECEMBER 15, 1906

William Hurd Lawrence
DECEMBER 22, 1906

Paul Bransom
JANUARY 5, 1907

Harrison Fisher
JANUARY 12, 1907

Grace Gebbie Wiederseim
JANUARY 19, 1907

Harrison Fisher
JANUARY 26, 1907

Harrison Fisher
FEBRUARY 2, 1907

Sarah Stilwell-Weber
FEBRUARY 9, 1907

Paul Bransom
FEBRUARY 16, 1907

Guernsey Moore
FEBRUARY 23, 1907

Guernsey Moore
MARCH 9, 1907

F. Rogers
MARCH 16, 1907

J. C. Leyendecker
MARCH 23, 1907

Harrison Fisher
MARCH 30, 1907

J. C. Leyendecker
APRIL 6, 1907

Harrison Fisher
APRIL 13, 1907

Artist unknown
APRIL 20, 1907

Sarah Stilwell-Weber
APRIL 27, 1907

Harry B. Lachman
MAY 4, 1907

Edward Penfield
MAY 11, 1907

Harrison Fisher
MAY 18, 1907

Harrison Fisher
MAY 25, 1907

J. J. Gould
JUNE 1, 1907

Edward Penfield
JUNE 8, 1907

Philip Boileau
JUNE 15, 1907

Oliver Kemp
JUNE 22, 1907

J. C. Leyendecker
JUNE 29, 1907

J. C. Leyendecker
JULY 6, 1907

Harrison Fisher
JULY 13, 1907

J. C. Leyendecker
JULY 20, 1907

Frank X. Leyendecker
JULY 27, 1907

George Brehm
AUGUST 3, 1907

Alonzo Kimball
AUGUST 10, 1907

Harrison Fisher
AUGUST 24, 1907

J. C. Leyendecker
AUGUST 31, 1907

George Brehm
SEPTEMBER 7, 1907

Allan Gilbert
SEPTEMBER 14, 1907

J. C. Leyendecker
SEPTEMBER 21, 1907

J. A. Cahill
SEPTEMBER 28, 1907

J. C. Leyendecker
OCTOBER 5, 1907

Allan Gilbert
OCTOBER 12, 1907

George Brehm
OCTOBER 26, 1907

Harrison Fisher
NOVEMBER 2, 1907

Harry B. Lachman
NOVEMBER 9, 1907

Harrison Fisher
NOVEMBER 16, 1907

J. C. Leyendecker
NOVEMBER 23, 1907

N. C. Wyeth
NOVEMBER 30, 1907

J. C. Leyendecker
DECEMBER 7, 1907

Oliver Kemp
DECEMBER 14, 1907

Artist unknown
DECEMBER 21, 1907

Stanley M. Arthurs
JANUARY 4, 1908

Frank X. Leyendecker
JANUARY 11, 1908

Harrison Fisher
JANUARY 18, 1908

Will Grefe
JANUARY 25, 1908

J. J. Gould
FEBRUARY 1, 1908

Alonzo Kimball
FEBRUARY 8, 1908

Ethel Franklin Betts
FEBRUARY 15, 1908

N. C. Wyeth
FEBRUARY 22, 1908

J. C. Leyendecker
FEBRUARY 29, 1908

Harrison Fisher
MARCH 7, 1908

George Brehm
MARCH 14, 1908

F. R. Gruger
MARCH 21, 1908

Alonzo Kimball
MARCH 28, 1908

J. C. Leyendecker
APRIL 4, 1908

J. C. Leyendecker
APRIL 11, 1908

Edmund Frederick
APRIL 18, 1908

Harrison Fisher
APRIL 25, 1908

Oliver Kemp
MAY 2, 1908

Harrison Fisher
MAY 9, 1908

James Montgomery Flagg
MAY 16, 1908

J. C. Leyendecker
MAY 23, 1908

Oliver Kemp
MAY 30, 1908

Worth Brehm
JUNE 6, 1908

Harrison Fisher
JUNE 13, 1908

Eugenie Wireman
JUNE 27, 1908

J. C. Leyendecker
JULY 4, 1908

Guernsey Moore
JULY 11, 1908

N. C. Wyeth
JULY 18, 1908

Harrison Fisher
JULY 25, 1908

Artist unknown
AUGUST 1, 1908

Sarah Stilwell-Weber
AUGUST 8, 1908

Harrison Fisher
AUGUST 15, 1908

Alonzo Kimball
AUGUST 22, 1908

Harrison Fisher
AUGUST 29, 1908

Sarah Stilwell-Weber
SEPTEMBER 5, 1908

J. C. Leyendecker
SEPTEMBER 12, 1908

F. Graham Cootes
SEPTEMBER 19, 1908

N. C. Wyeth
SEPTEMBER 26, 1908

Sarah Stilwell-Weber
OCTOBER 3, 1908

Harrison Fisher
OCTOBER 10, 1908

Clarence Underwood
OCTOBER 17, 1908

Alonzo Kimball
OCTOBER 24, 1908

Harrison Fisher
NOVEMBER 7, 1908

J. C. Leyendecker
NOVEMBER 14, 1908

J. C. Leyendecker
NOVEMBER 21, 1908

Harrison Fisher
NOVEMBER 28, 1908

Sarah Stilwell-Weber
DECEMBER 5, 1908

J. C. Leyendecker
DECEMBER 19, 1908

J. C. Leyendecker
JANUARY 2, 1909

Harrison Fisher
JANUARY 9, 1909

J. C. Leyendecker
JANUARY 16, 1909

Henrietta Adams
JANUARY 23, 1909

Henry Hutt
JANUARY 30, 1909

Harrison Fisher
FEBRUARY 6, 1909

Sarah Stilwell-Weber
FEBRUARY 13, 1909

Alonzo Kimball
FEBRUARY 20, 1909

Oliver Kemp
FEBRUARY 27, 1909

Paul Bransom
MARCH 13, 1909

Philip Boileau
MARCH 20, 1909

Harrison Fisher
MARCH 27, 1909

J. C. Leyendecker
APRIL 3, 1909

J. C. Leyendecker
APRIL 10, 1909

Harrison Fisher
APRIL 17, 1909

Grace Gebbie Wiederseim
APRIL 24, 1909

Oliver Kemp
MAY 1, 1909

Harrison Fisher
MAY 8, 1909

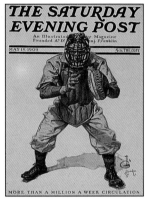

J. C. Leyendecker
MAY 15, 1909

Will Grefe
MAY 22, 1909

Alonzo Kimball
MAY 29, 1909

Worth Brehm
JUNE 5, 1909

Philip Boileau
JUNE 12, 1909

Harrison Fisher
JUNE 26, 1909

Stanley M. Arthurs
JULY 10, 1909

Harrison Fisher
JULY 17, 1909

Harrison Fisher
JULY 24, 1909

Charles Livingston Bull
JULY 31, 1909

Harrison Fisher
AUGUST 7, 1909

Edward Penfield
AUGUST 14, 1909

Sarah Stilwell-Weber
AUGUST 21, 1909

Harrison Fisher
AUGUST 28, 1909

F. S. Manning
SEPTEMBER 4, 1909

Walter H. Everett
SEPTEMBER 11, 1909

J. C. Leyendecker
SEPTEMBER 18, 1909

Harrison Fisher
SEPTEMBER 25, 1909

Sarah Stilwell-Weber
OCTOBER 9, 1909

Oliver Kemp
OCTOBER 16, 1909

Fousey
OCTOBER 23, 1909

Philip Boileau
NOVEMBER 6, 1909

Carol Aus
NOVEMBER 20, 1909

Harrison Fisher
NOVEMBER 27, 1909

J. C. Leyendecker
DECEMBER 4, 1909

Harrison Fisher
DECEMBER 11, 1909

Sarah Stilwell-Weber
DECEMBER 25, 1909

Sarah Stilwell-Weber
JANUARY 29, 1910

Sarah Stilwell-Weber
APRIL 9, 1910

J. C. Leyendecker
SEPTEMBER 10, 1910

J. C. Leyendecker
FEBRUARY 25, 1911

CHAPTER 2

1910–1919

Even before August 1914 and the outbreak of what Americans at first called the "European war," the *Saturday Evening Post* was growing in power and influence. A number of the themes and ideas that had been central to the development of the *Post* in the first decade of the century were now abandoned in favor of more current interests. Changes inside the magazine were reflected on the covers. Themes once popular for cover illustrations disappeared as new graphic ideas were explored. And just as new and important writers were introduced in the magazine, so the work of new artists began appearing on the covers, with new styles and, in some cases, new subject matter.

Of the four major artists from the first decade, only J. C. Leyendecker remained a frequent contributor. Leyendecker, in fact, was the *Post*'s preeminent illustrator during these years, painting well over one hundred covers. He continued to experiment with a variety of subjects and attitudes, but his most noteworthy work marked and celebrated America's holidays: Valentine's Day, Easter, the Fourth of July, Halloween, Thanksgiving, Christmas, and the New Year. He painted covers for all these holidays in this period and some, like the Fourth of July and the New Year, belonged to him exclusively.

Leyendecker's New Year's baby undertook a variety of activities in the years before the war. Sometimes these covers were topical. For example, in 1910 the Leyendecker baby was shown flying a dual stick airplane, and in 1912 a girl baby touted "Votes for Women." Sometimes the illustration hit on more conventional ideas, as in 1913 when the baby turned to a clean page in a large book to write "Resolved." Occasionally, the cover simply advertised the *Post*: in 1911 the baby appeared with a *Post* bag on his shoulder, selling a copy of the magazine to Father Time.

At the very beginning of the decade the Leyendecker baby still showed up on holidays other than the New Year. In 1910, he—or she—helped the mailman deliver valentines, tried on a flowered hat for Easter, and leaped away from an exploding July Fourth firecracker. By the next year, the baby had become reserved for the New Year, and Leyendecker drew other characters for other holidays. Often these were children, typically little boys, as in 1910 when Leyendecker used a boy digging into his turkey dinner for Thanksgiving, and two years later, virtually the same boy eagerly watching his mother baste the turkey. Sometimes the character changed but the theme remained constant. Thus, in 1911, the firecracker theme was employed again for the Fourth of July, but now a small boy grinned as he prepared to light the firecracker at the foot of an unwitting policeman (top right, page 45). In 1912, another small boy was shown suffering from his own unhappy encounter with a firecracker as his grandmother treated his burned finger (bottom left, page 45). Less frequently, Leyendecker painted little girls. A girl and a boy appeared together for July 5, 1913; both wore paper tricorn hats and saluted, the girl holding a flag and the boy a sword. And for Christmas that same year, a little girl mailed a letter to Santa Claus.

Some of Leyendecker's covers were comic or whimsical, and babies and children suited that tone well. Other covers assumed different tones: sentimental or elegant or even baroque. In these cases, he typically worked with adult characters. Old folks were sometimes treated sentimentally. For Flag Day in 1913, he painted two old men at a parade, one holding a flag and the other playing a fife. The same year, a comically over-elegant young man celebrated Easter on the *Post* cover. Leyendecker's ornate cycle is exemplified by his December 2, 1911, illustration (bottom right, page 45) of a butler bearing a tray with a suckling pig.

In the first years of the decade, before the Great War, *Post* covers continued to find in women their most popular image. Harrison Fisher drew women for the magazine, as did Philip Boileau and Clarence Underwood. In addition, a number of new artists added their portraits of women, among them W. Haskell Coffin, Z. P. Nikolaki, Neysa McMein, and Penrhyn Stanlaws.

Fisher and Underwood excelled in romantic portraits of lovely women. Fish-

J. C. Leyendecker
DECEMBER 3, 1910

J. C. Leyendecker
JULY 1, 1911

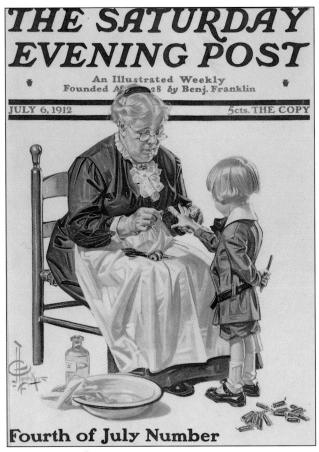

J. C. Leyendecker
JULY 6, 1912

J. C. Leyendecker
DECEMBER 2, 1911

45

er's paintings presented beautiful young women, posed and static, often with a minor prop—perhaps an engagement ring or a kitten. For the Christmas cover for 1910 (top left, page 48) he drew a woman with holly in her hair, holding a rose.

Underwood, by contrast, enhanced his portraits with suggestions of action. His elegant women were often engaged in sports, or so the combination of costume and prop suggested. In 1910, he drew a woman in sailing costume at the tiller of an implied boat (September 3). The next year, he painted a woman on a sled (March 4, 1911). On June 15, 1912, an Underwood cover showed a woman, her sleeves rolled up, at the wheel of a racing car. Such covers seemed to applaud the idea of the "New Woman," but fundamentally, Underwood's work, like Harrison Fisher's, simply celebrated female beauty. How casually Underwood exploited such feminist goals as women's suffrage can be seen in his cover for October 19, 1912 (top right, page 48). Captioned "Her First Ballot," the cover looked ahead to the November election, the first in which women could vote. But the woman Underwood painted for the cover is not shown voting; with her ballot before her, she is taking the opportunity to powder her nose.

W. Haskell Coffin, whose work for the *Post* began in 1913, also contributed to the number of beautiful women featured on the covers. His special touch was to depict them caught in some minimal action— a woman holds her hat against a sudden wind on the March 13, 1915, cover (bottom right, page 48)—or in some whimsical pose; a bird perches on a woman's finger on the July 31, 1915, issue. Other Coffin covers, like those of Fisher and Underwood, simply featured a beautiful model in a beautiful costume, in one case in an evening cloak carrying a fan (December 13, 1913).

Philip Boileau continued his typical work, close-up paintings of women's faces, but he varied these with portraits of women with children, usually girls, or with some attractive prop—for example, a vase of dogwood branches (June 17, 1911). Portraits were also Penrhyn Stanlaws's specialty. Typical examples include a woman with a muff or a woman, in profile, wearing a bonnet (January 10, 1914, and September 27, 1913). Neysa McMein's paintings of women were often enhanced with the suggestions of a setting; on the March 17, 1917, cover an ice-cream soda implied a soda fountain. When America entered the war, McMein was able, as we shall see, to use this kind of suggestion to particularly good effect.

Z. P. Nikolaki (also known as N. P. Zarokilli), who began his career with the *Post* in 1911, brought a rather different style to its covers. His women were not even distantly related to the American girl, whose various incarnations the other illustrators typically represented. The exotic beauties of Nikolaki were much more striking, and subtly more erotic. He often worked on a regal theme, in one instance painting a young woman on a thronelike chair (February 27, 1915; bottom left, page 48). Exotic and even outré costumes were another favorite device, as on the February 8, 1913, cover, showing a woman in harlequin dress carrying a guitar. As with McMein and others, the war would provide Nikolaki with interesting possibilities for varying his portraits.

The cover work of Sarah Stilwell-Weber featured almost exclusively pictures of lovely children, mostly girls—juvenile counterparts of the women of Fisher, Underwood, Boileau, and others. Like the painters of women, Stilwell-Weber set her little girls in evocative settings or provided them with a simple prop that emphasized their female innocence. Early examples from 1910 include a girl dressed in a fur hat and a muff, carrying ice skates (top left, page 42); another flying a kite (top right, page 42); and a third watering roses (January 29, April 9, and June 11). Stilwell-Weber's covers often emphasized the seasons. The April 15, 1911, cover set a little girl amid flowers and butterflies; for October 14 of that year, children played in fallen leaves.

Portraits of women and little girls continued to dominate *Post* covers as earlier thematic illustrations disappeared. No longer did the covers feature paintings in support of stories in the issue, and the attempt to depict business themes petered out, as did representations of the West. But in the years before the war, a new approach to cover art made its appearance, an approach that would come to typify *Post* covers and, indeed, the *Post* itself.

That new approach might best be called narrative illustration, and the greatest practitioner of this form was Norman Rockwell, whose first *Post* cover appeared May 20, 1916. But Rockwell had predecessors, other artists who had been experimenting with narrative illustration as early as 1910.

The extraordinarily versatile Leyendecker explored the possibilities of narrative most often in paintings centered on figures of children, usually boys. For September 10, 1910, he told the story of the opening of school with a cover showing two boys: one is dressed for school, carrying his books; the other is barefoot, carrying a fishing pole (bottom left, page 42). Early in 1911 he painted boys in a snowball fight (February 25; bottom right, page 42); two years later, he drew a small group of children putting on a show or a circus for their peers (July 19, 1913).

New *Post* artists were also working out the possibilities of narrative, the most important of them being Robert Robinson,

Charles A. MacLellan, and Leslie Thrasher. Like Leyendecker, these illustrators featured children, typically boys, and exploited the comic elements of their play. These artists also turned to old people for ideas, again emphasizing the humorous side. On the covers of the *Post* there were now two distinct worlds: women and little girls had come to represent the glow of sentiment and romance, while old people and little boys provided the fun.

Robert Robinson's most important work featured variations on a rural man, an "old codger" or "geezer." At first, Robinson painted him in typically rural settings, sometimes merely dealing with the weather. Sometimes Robinson placed his figure in slightly more complex settings, emphasizing the narrative implications. The November 26, 1910, cover finds the old man at the stove of the general store regarding an election poster (left, page 54). The same theme is developed more successfully two years later, with a cover showing a politician campaigning in the countryside, handing his card and a cigar to a skeptical old farmer (November 2, 1912).

In his most interesting work, Robinson found ways to bring his old codger into contact with modern times, allowing the inherent contrast to carry the comic elements of the implied story. The January 11, 1913, cover showed an old couple driving; the man is delighted to be spinning along, but his wife is filled with anxiety and grips both her hat and his arm. In 1914 Robinson took his old codger to a museum and placed him face to face with a Cubist painting (June 27; right, page 54). Later that year, the same figure watches airplanes through a pair of field glasses, his mouth agape in astonishment (July 18).

Charles A. MacLellan, like Robinson, did some paintings of old folks, but his more

Harrison Fisher
DECEMBER 24, 1910

Clarence F. Underwood
OCTOBER 19, 1912

N. P. Zarokilli
FEBRUARY 27, 1915

William Haskell Coffin
MARCH 13, 1915

memorable covers were those with children, again typically boys. Often these boys are in some kind of trouble, but it's the kind of trouble that makes the viewer smile. For example, the September 7, 1912, cover shows a schoolboy and his teacher, who has just discovered that the boy has carved his initials in the desk. A similar cover the next year features a father discovering his son's picture of him on a slate; the picture is not flattering (April 5, 1913). The tables are turned in 1915: a boy smirks as his dad, unsuccessfully, tries to help out with the homework (November 6).

Leslie Thrasher, too, worked with both oldsters and children, and his principal work was with boys as well. An early cover, June 8, 1912, presented a small group of ragamuffins playing baseball, but his later work grew more explicitly comic. For Christmas 1914, he drew a boy downcast with disappointment as he discovers in his Christmas stocking a copy of *Lives of the Saints* (December 26). A year later a Thrasher boy, seated beside a starchy woman, pats the dog he has sneaked into church, and in another instance lies wide-eyed in bed, long after bedtime, reading a thrilling story (October 16 and December 4, 1915).

When Norman Rockwell's first cover appeared on the *Post*, it was a work that clearly imitated, and in many ways improved on, the comic narrative illustrations already so popular. In fact, that famous first cover, showing a miserable boy wheeling the family's new baby in a carriage to the undisguised amusement of his friends, was simply Rockwell's version of a cover painted by MacLellan for August 2, 1913. MacLellan presented a disgruntled boy pushing a baby in a carriage; Rockwell added the chorus of bystanders. Another very early Rockwell cover, for June 3, 1916,

echoed an earlier work by Leyendecker: the children's show or circus. Rockwell improved on Leyendecker's idea, placing the boys in specific roles, one as a barker and another as a strongman. Beginning in what was already a familiar vein, the comic illustration featuring boys, Rockwell would take the narrative in entirely new directions, extending both the range of characters and the emotional tone of his illustrations. But those developments lay ahead.

When the European war broke out in August 1914, the *Post*, committed to neutrality, sent several of its most important writers to the front. On the home front, writers turned their attention to the war in various ways: business writers wrote about the effect of war on business; health writers provided features on the health hazards of modern warfare; fiction writers attempted to bring the war into stories of adventure or romance. Similarly, cover artists turned to war themes, finding ways to carry the theme of war into their illustrations of beautiful women or winsome children or comic oldsters or humorous boys.

The *Post* first presented war images on its covers in October. The first of these was the work of Leyendecker. For October 3 he drew a picture of Uncle Sam reading a newspaper with the headline "Big Battle Rages" (top left, page 52). Penrhyn Stanlaws followed the next week with an approach that would become a common one: the beautiful woman painted with some aspect of costume or prop that gestured toward the idea of war. For this cover, Stanlaws drew a woman in a Red Cross uniform. Leyendecker returned on October 24 with a particularly memorable painting: a Belgian peasant woman sits at a rude table; her head has fallen to the table and from her hand has fallen a letter, presumably a notice of the death of her son. Beside her stands a small, bewildered peasant girl. The final cover of the month was the work of Walter Everett, showing a French soldier and a dead horse.

The flurry of war covers in October was short-lived. Editor Lorimer did not intend to devote his magazine to a war he detested and considered barbaric. He soon recalled the *Post* writers he had sent to Europe, and coverage of the war was minimized during 1915 and 1916. Occasional articles and stories featured the war, as did the occasional cover, but for the most part cover artists continued to mine familiar veins.

The few exceptions are worth consideration. Leyendecker used his New Year's baby to express his, and Lorimer's, antiwar sentiments. On January 2, 1915, the Leyendecker baby briskly sweeps away a litter of European military helmets. Six weeks later Leyendecker drew a Scots soldier writing a letter; the soldier's head is bandaged and his foot is placed on a piece of enemy artillery he has destroyed (February 13). With one other exception *Post* covers for 1915 stayed away from war themes. The exception is a painting by Guernsey Moore, whose work had been absent from the covers of the magazine for several years. Moore did a cover for August 21, featuring a British, French, and Belgian soldier, standing together in a manly pose and backed by half-furled flags (top right, page 52).

In 1916, as Woodrow Wilson ran for reelection on the strength of having kept the country out of war, the *Post* again featured only a small number of war-inspired covers. Leyendecker celebrated July 4 with a painting of Uncle Sam, this time armed with a carbine. And at the end of the year, he placed his New Year's baby in an ominous setting, regarding a globe with a hole blown out where Europe had once been (December 30).

On April 6, 1917, the United States declared that a state of war existed with Germany. Lorimer, like most of the country, had been practicing preparedness and with the April 21 issue the *Post*, too, declared war. Charles Livingston Bull, the famous nature illustrator, was commissioned to paint the cover for this issue. Bull used a vivid orange-red wash against which he painted the American eagle, talons extended, swooping down on an unseen enemy (bottom left, page 52). For the next year and a half, war dominated the covers of the magazine.

Much like the *Post*'s fiction writers, the cover illustrators had to discover ways to represent the war, for this was unfamiliar terrain. The most convenient adjustment, as mentioned above, was simply recostuming a beautiful woman or shifting the props with which she was drawn. Neysa McMein did a number of such covers: one woman makes bandages, another wears a flyer's helmet with goggles, a third appears as a Red Cross nurse (May 26 and August 11, 1917; August 31, 1918). Nikolaki's women, too, were recast in war roles. The July 28, 1917, cover presented a lovely woman standing before a mirror to adjust her Red Cross headgear. Clarence Underwood painted a cover with a woman reading a letter from a soldier, the censor's stamp prominently displayed (June 8, 1918). A new artist, J. Knowles Hare, drew a woman in a canteen uniform serving coffee and sandwiches, and in another instance showed a woman preparing to launch a ship with a bottle of champagne (August 3 and November 9, 1918). Sarah Stilwell-Weber's girls underwent similar transformations. One appears in the now-familiar Red Cross headgear, diligently knitting; another wreathes daisies around a service star (July 13 and October 5, 1918).

The narrative, especially the comic narrative, was also turned to war purposes.

For the June 16, 1917, cover Rockwell painted two boys, one playing the part of a recruiting sergeant and the other of a would-be recruit who fails to measure up to the prescribed height (bottom right, page 52). A few months later, on September 15, Charles MacLellan played on a similar theme, with a boy sergeant drilling three boy recruits. Robert Robinson drew a schoolboy in trouble with his teacher; this time the problem is that the boy is daydreaming, imagining himself in uniform carrying a handful of German helmets as trophies of his military prowess (October 12, 1918).

Oldsters, too, found their way into war covers. Another new artist, Harold Matthews Brett, did a cover for January 12, 1918, that showed an old couple seated together, with the man's arm around his wife. He looks at their photograph album while she holds a picture of their soldier son and stares off into the distance. Later that year, Robinson painted a somewhat younger but clearly middle-aged couple. Together they read a newspaper that tells of a local boy winning the Croix de Guerre; the photograph in the paper echoes the picture of their son on the wall (September 7; top right, page 53).

Every one of these themes, and a good many more, were tried out by Leyendecker, whose work during the war years demonstrated the breadth of his imagination and the flexibility of his style. Of course, each year began with the personal comment on the war made by the New Year's baby. At the end of 1916 he had been dismayed at the exploding globe, but by the close of 1917, he stood naked in a helmet, carrying a sword and proudly saluting (December 29). A year later, Leyendecker's baby released a dove from a cage (December 28, 1918; bottom left, page 53). Framed by images of war

and peace, the Leyendecker covers for the *Post* provided Americans with a variety of images that ranged through the ideas and emotions evoked by the war.

As early as May 19, 1917, Leyendecker showed America what patriotism and sacrifice looked like. A young husband has enlisted; in uniform, he embraces his wife as he departs for France. For June 30, he wove together the current war and the spirit of '76: with the somewhat spectral figure of George Washington mounted behind them, three doughboys, their bayonets ready, rush into action. But the American soldier is not only a brave fighter, he is also a friend of the war-oppressed. On September 22, Leyendecker's doughboy, armed with an English-French phrase book, tries to communicate with a little peasant girl. Two weeks later, he writes a letter home by the light of a campfire (October 6). Between the middle of November and the end of the year, five more Leyendecker covers appeared, ending of course with the New Year's baby. In one, an old woman knits and thinks; she wears a pin carrying the portrait of a sailor (November 10). On the December 8 cover, a jaunty soldier marches along with a plum pudding in his hand and a sprig of holly in his mess kit. For Christmas, he shares his bread with a Belgian girl (December 22).

Leyendecker's imagination was not exhausted, for he continued to produce new and evocative war covers throughout 1918. Some were simply patriotic affirmations of America. For March 2, he painted a cover that became a famous war bond poster: a formidable figure of Liberty stands before us, carrying a shield; under her protection is a proud Boy Scout, armed with a sword (top left, page 53). For the Fourth of July, he produced a spirit of '76 drummer (July 6). But other covers were more complex. In one, an old woman, with shawl and prayer

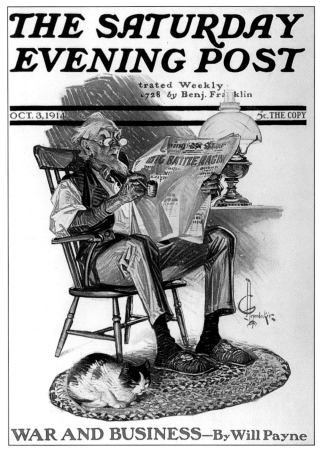

J. C. Leyendecker
OCTOBER 3, 1914

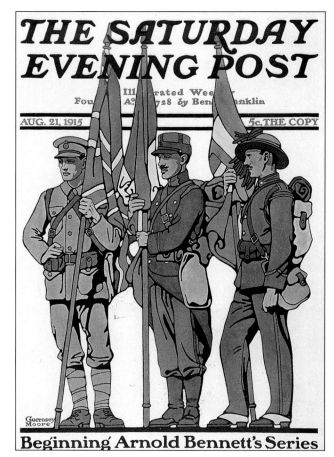

Guernsey Moore
AUGUST 21, 1915

Charles Livingston Bull
APRIL 21, 1917

Norman Rockwell
JUNE 16, 1917

J. C. Leyendecker
MARCH 2, 1918

Robert Robinson
SEPTEMBER 7, 1918

J. C. Leyendecker
DECEMBER 28, 1918

Charles A. MacLellan
FEBRUARY 8, 1919

53

book, kneels in church; beside her, kneeling but erect, a young sailor looks, open-eyed, into the future (March 23). A week later, Leyendecker gave the *Post* the standard beautiful woman, another Red Cross nurse, this time ornamented with a pot of tulips (March 30). Both men and women could be stalwart and heroic: for July 27, Leyendecker painted a doughboy as he hurled a grenade over the wall of a trench, and for August 17, a woman wearing the badge of the Motor Corps proudly salutes.

Leyendecker's range of tone is dramatically evident in his work at the very end of the war. At one extreme is a remarkably moving painting for October 26. A young Belgian woman refugee, wearing the traditional sabots, labors between the traces of a cart she is hauling; the cart is loaded with all the household goods that remain, and on top of them sits her very small son, who holds a birdcage. The old family dog, tied to the traces, pulls along with her. A jauntier Leyendecker greeted the holidays. For the Thanksgiving issue on November 30, a cheery doughboy led a turkey on a string; and on December 7, Santa in a red coat and uniform, the Bible under his arm, saluted.

With Leyendecker's baby releasing the dove of peace, the *Post*'s war was over. Only a rare reference to the war remained, and the last word is best left to Charles MacLellan, who, for the cover of February 8, 1919, painted one of his comic oldsters, a rural man driving his sleigh home; beside him in the sleigh is his uniformed son, home at last from France (bottom right, page 53).

Robert Robinson
NOVEMBER 26, 1910

Robert Robinson
JUNE 27, 1914

J. C. Leyendecker
JANUARY 1, 1910

Robert Robinson
JANUARY 8, 1910

Harrison Fisher
JANUARY 15, 1910

Walter H. Everett
JANUARY 22, 1910

Harrison Fisher
FEBRUARY 5, 1910

J. C. Leyendecker
FEBRUARY 12, 1910

Robert Robinson
FEBRUARY 19, 1910

F. Graham Cootes
FEBRUARY 26, 1910

Harrison Fisher
MARCH 5, 1910

Sarah Stilwell-Weber
MARCH 12, 1910

Worth Brehm
MARCH 19, 1910

J. C. Leyendecker
MARCH 26, 1910

Harrison Fisher
APRIL 2, 1910

Anton Otto Fischer
APRIL 16, 1910

Philip Boileau
APRIL 23, 1910

Frank X. Leyendecker
APRIL 30, 1910

Carol Aus
MAY 7, 1910

Anton Otto Fischer
MAY 14, 1910

Harrison Fisher
MAY 21, 1910

Robert Robinson
MAY 28, 1910

J. C. Leyendecker
JUNE 4, 1910

Sarah Stilwell-Weber
JUNE 11, 1910

Walter H. Everett
JUNE 18, 1910

Carol Aus
JUNE 25, 1910

J. C. Leyendecker
JULY 2, 1910

Robert Robinson
JULY 9, 1910

Harrison Fisher
JULY 16, 1910

Anton Otto Fischer
JULY 23, 1910

Carol Aus
JULY 30, 1910

J. C. Leyendecker
AUGUST 6, 1910

Henry Hutt
AUGUST 13, 1910

Sarah Stilwell-Weber
AUGUST 20, 1910

Edna Longest
AUGUST 27, 1910

Clarence Underwood
SEPTEMBER 3, 1910

Oliver Kemp
SEPTEMBER 17, 1910

Carol Aus
SEPTEMBER 24, 1910

Robert Robinson
OCTOBER 1, 1910

Philip Boileau
OCTOBER 8, 1910

Robert Robinson
OCTOBER 15, 1910

Harrison Fisher
OCTOBER 22, 1910

Sarah Stilwell-Weber
OCTOBER 29, 1910

Harrison Fisher
NOVEMBER 5, 1910

J. C. Leyendecker
NOVEMBER 12, 1910

Philip Boileau
NOVEMBER 19, 1910

Harrison Fisher
DECEMBER 10, 1910

Robert Robinson
DECEMBER 17, 1910

J. C. Leyendecker
DECEMBER 31, 1910

Sarah Stilwell-Weber
JANUARY 7, 1911

F. Earl Christy
JANUARY 14, 1911

Robert Robinson
JANUARY 21, 1911

Sarah Stilwell-Weber
JANUARY 28, 1911

Harrison Fisher
FEBRUARY 4, 1911

Anton Otto Fischer
FEBRUARY 11, 1911

Clarence F. Underwood
FEBRUARY 18, 1911

Clarence F. Underwood
MARCH 4, 1911

Alonzo Kimball
MARCH 11, 1911

Robert Robinson
MARCH 18, 1911

Z. P. Nikolaki
MARCH 25, 1911

J. C. Leyendecker
APRIL 1, 1911

Harrison Fisher
APRIL 8, 1911

Sarah Stilwell-Weber
APRIL 15, 1911

Robert Robinson
APRIL 22, 1911

Frank X. Leyendecker
APRIL 29, 1911

Philip Boileau
MAY 6, 1911

Robert Robinson
MAY 13, 1911

Sarah Stilwell-Weber
MAY 20, 1911

Harrison Fisher
MAY 27, 1911

Robert Robinson
JUNE 3, 1911

Eugenie M. Wireman
JUNE 10, 1911

Philip Boileau
JUNE 17, 1911

Robert Robinson
JUNE 24, 1911

Sarah Stilwell-Weber
JULY 8, 1911

Harrison Fisher
JULY 15, 1911

Robert Robinson
JULY 22, 1911

Chase Emerson
JULY 29, 1911

Harrison Fisher
AUGUST 5, 1911

Clarence F. Underwood
AUGUST 12, 1911

J. C. Leyendecker
AUGUST 19, 1911

The Kinneys
AUGUST 26, 1911

J. C. Leyendecker
SEPTEMBER 2, 1911

Philip Boileau
SEPTEMBER 9, 1911

Robert Robinson
SEPTEMBER 16, 1911

Clarence F. Underwood
SEPTEMBER 23, 1911

Robert Robinson
SEPTEMBER 30, 1911

Charles David Williams
OCTOBER 7, 1911

Sarah Stilwell-Weber
OCTOBER 14, 1911

Harrison Fisher
OCTOBER 21, 1911

Robert Robinson
OCTOBER 28, 1911

Philip Boileau
NOVEMBER 4, 1911

J. S. Campton
NOVEMBER 11, 1911

J. C. Leyendecker
NOVEMBER 18, 1911

Harrison Fisher
NOVEMBER 25, 1911

Robert Robinson
DECEMBER 9, 1911

Philip Boileau
DECEMBER 16, 1911

Clarence F. Underwood
DECEMBER 23, 1911

J. C. Leyendecker
DECEMBER 30, 1911

Clarence F. Underwood
JANUARY 6, 1912

Charles A. MacLellan
JANUARY 13, 1912

Harrison Fisher
JANUARY 20, 1912

Clarence F. Underwood
JANUARY 27, 1912

Philip Boileau
FEBRUARY 3, 1912

F. Graham Cootes
FEBRUARY 10, 1912

Harrison Fisher
FEBRUARY 17, 1912

Charles David Williams
FEBRUARY 24, 1912

Philip Boileau
MARCH 2, 1912

Clarence F. Underwood
MARCH 9, 1912

Charles A. MacLellan
MARCH 16, 1912

Charles David Williams
MARCH 23, 1912

N. P. Zarokilli
MARCH 30, 1912

J. C. Leyendecker
APRIL 6, 1912

Robert Robinson
APRIL 13, 1912

N. P. Zarokilli
APRIL 20, 1912

Charles A. MacLellan
APRIL 27, 1912

Robert Robinson
MAY 4, 1912

Philip Boileau
MAY 11, 1912

Harrison Fisher
MAY 18, 1912

J. C. Leyendecker
MAY 25, 1912

Olive Rush
JUNE 1, 1912

Leslie Thrasher
JUNE 8, 1912

Clarence F. Underwood
JUNE 15, 1912

Frank X. Leyendecker
JUNE 22, 1912

Harrison Fisher
JUNE 29, 1912

Anna Nordstrom Feind
JULY 13, 1912

Robert Robinson
JULY 20, 1912

Clarence F. Underwood
JULY 27, 1912

Leslie Thrasher
AUGUST 3, 1912

N. P. Zarokilli
AUGUST 10, 1912

Henry J. Soulen
AUGUST 17, 1912

Clarence F. Underwood
AUGUST 24, 1912

Philip Boileau
AUGUST 31, 1912

Charles A. MacLellan
SEPTEMBER 7, 1912

Robert Robinson
SEPTEMBER 14, 1912

Clarence F. Underwood
SEPTEMBER 21, 1912

Frank X. Leyendecker
SEPTEMBER 28, 1912

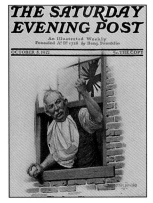

Leslie Thrasher
OCTOBER 5, 1912

Frank X. Leyendecker
OCTOBER 12, 1912

J. C. Leyendecker
OCTOBER 26, 1912

Robert Robinson
NOVEMBER 2, 1912

Clarence F. Underwood
NOVEMBER 9, 1912

J. C. Leyendecker
NOVEMBER 16, 1912

Philip Boileau
NOVEMBER 23, 1912

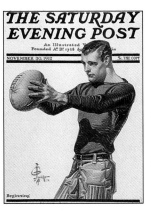

J. C. Leyendecker
NOVEMBER 30, 1912

J. C. Leyendecker
DECEMBER 7, 1912

Harrison Fisher
DECEMBER 14, 1912

Clarence F. Underwood
DECEMBER 21, 1912

J. C. Leyendecker
DECEMBER 28, 1912

N. P. Zarokilli
JANUARY 4, 1913

Clarence F. Underwood
JANUARY 18, 1913

Philip Boileau
JANUARY 25, 1913

Carol Aus
FEBRUARY 1, 1913

N. P. Zarokilli
FEBRUARY 8, 1913

Charles A. MacLellan
FEBRUARY 15, 1913

Charles David Williams
FEBRUARY 22, 1913

Philip Boileau
MARCH 1, 1913

Clarence F. Underwood
MARCH 8, 1913

Robert Robinson
MARCH 15, 1913

J. C. Leyendecker
MARCH 22, 1913

Henry J. Soulen
MARCH 29, 1913

Charles A. MacLellan
APRIL 5, 1913

Clarence F. Underwood
APRIL 12, 1913

Philip Boileau
APRIL 19, 1913

Robert Robinson
APRIL 26, 1913

Carol Aus
MAY 3, 1913

Clarence F. Underwood
MAY 10, 1913

Robert Robinson
MAY 17, 1913

J. C. Leyendecker
MAY 24, 1913

Clarence F. Underwood
MAY 31, 1913

Philip Boileau
JUNE 7, 1913

Violet Moore Higgins
JUNE 14, 1913

J. C. Leyendecker
JUNE 21, 1913

Charles David Williams
JUNE 28, 1913

J. C. Leyendecker
JULY 5, 1913

Philip Boileau
JULY 12, 1913

J. C. Leyendecker
JULY 19, 1913

Penrhyn Stanlaws
JULY 26, 1913

Charles A. MacLellan
AUGUST 2, 1913

Philip Boileau
AUGUST 9, 1913

Clarence F. Underwood
AUGUST 16, 1913

William Haskell Coffin
AUGUST 23, 1913

Penrhyn Stanlaws
AUGUST 30, 1913

Leslie Thrasher
SEPTEMBER 6, 1913

Charles A. MacLellan
SEPTEMBER 13, 1913

J. C. Leyendecker
SEPTEMBER 20, 1913

Penrhyn Stanlaws
SEPTEMBER 27, 1913

Clarence F. Underwood
OCTOBER 4, 1913

William Haskell Coffin
OCTOBER 11, 1913

Charles A. MacLellan
OCTOBER 18, 1913

Penrhyn Stanlaws
OCTOBER 25, 1913

J. C. Leyendecker
NOVEMBER 1, 1913

Chase Emerson
NOVEMBER 8, 1913

J. C. Leyendecker
NOVEMBER 15, 1913

Clarence F. Underwood
NOVEMBER 22, 1913

J. C. Leyendecker
NOVEMBER 29, 1913

Charles A. MacLellan
DECEMBER 6, 1913

William Haskell Coffin
DECEMBER 13, 1913

J. C. Leyendecker
DECEMBER 20, 1913

Philip Boileau
DECEMBER 27, 1913

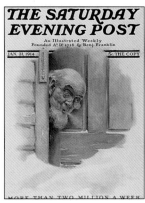

J. C. Leyendecker
JANUARY 3, 1914

Penrhyn Stanlaws
JANUARY 10, 1914

Charles A. MacLellan
JANUARY 17, 1914

Penrhyn Stanlaws
JANUARY 24, 1914

Robert Robinson
JANUARY 31, 1914

Clarence F. Underwood
FEBRUARY 7, 1914

Penrhyn Stanlaws
FEBRUARY 14, 1914

Philip Boileau
FEBRUARY 21, 1914

Leslie Thrasher
FEBRUARY 28, 1914

Clarence F. Underwood
MARCH 7, 1914

Charles A. MacLellan
MARCH 14, 1914

Penrhyn Stanlaws
MARCH 21, 1914

Charles A. MacLellan
MARCH 28, 1914

William Haskell Coffin
APRIL 4, 1914

J. C. Leyendecker
APRIL 11, 1914

Robert Robinson
APRIL 18, 1914

J. C. Leyendecker
APRIL 25, 1914

Sarah Stilwell-Weber
MAY 2, 1914

Penrhyn Stanlaws
MAY 9, 1914

Leslie Thrasher
MAY 16, 1914

William Haskell Coffin
MAY 23, 1914

J. C. Leyendecker
MAY 30, 1914

Leslie Thrasher
JUNE 6, 1914

J. C. Leyendecker
JUNE 13, 1914

William Haskell Coffin
JUNE 20, 1914

J. C. Leyendecker
JULY 4, 1914

Philip Boileau
JULY 11, 1914

Robert Robinson
JULY 18, 1914

William Haskell Coffin
JULY 25, 1914

Sarah Stilwell-Weber
AUGUST 1, 1914

Leslie Thrasher
AUGUST 8, 1914

Penrhyn Stanlaws
AUGUST 15, 1914

Frank X. Leyendecker
AUGUST 22, 1914

Penrhyn Stanlaws
AUGUST 29, 1914

Leslie Thrasher
SEPTEMBER 5, 1914

C. H. Taffs
SEPTEMBER 12, 1914

J. C. Leyendecker
SEPTEMBER 19, 1914

Philip Boileau
SEPTEMBER 26, 1914

Penrhyn Stanlaws
OCTOBER 10, 1914

Sarah Stilwell-Weber
OCTOBER 17, 1914

J. C. Leyendecker
OCTOBER 24, 1914

Walter H. Everett
OCTOBER 31, 1914

Sarah Stilwell-Weber
NOVEMBER 7, 1914

Francis Miller
NOVEMBER 14, 1914

J. C. Leyendecker
NOVEMBER 21, 1914

J. C. Leyendecker
NOVEMBER 28, 1914

Sarah Stilwell-Weber
DECEMBER 5, 1914

Philip Boileau
DECEMBER 12, 1914

J. C. Leyendecker
DECEMBER 19, 1914

Leslie Thrasher
DECEMBER 26, 1914

J. C. Leyendecker
JANUARY 2, 1915

N. P. Zarokilli
JANUARY 9, 1915

Philip Boileau
JANUARY 16, 1915

Leslie Thrasher
JANUARY 23, 1915

N. P. Zarokilli
JANUARY 30, 1915

Charles Frederick Naegele
FEBRUARY 6, 1915

Walter H. Everett
FEBRUARY 13, 1915

Charles A. MacLellan
FEBRUARY 20, 1915

Leslie Thrasher
MARCH 6, 1915

Penrhyn Stanlaws
MARCH 20, 1915

Philip Boileau
MARCH 27, 1915

J. C. Leyendecker
APRIL 3, 1915

C. Warde Traver
APRIL 10, 1915

William Haskell Coffin
APRIL 17, 1915

John A. Coughlin
APRIL 24, 1915

Sarah Stilwell-Weber
MAY 1, 1915

William Haskell Coffin
MAY 8, 1915

Sarah Stilwell-Weber
MAY 15, 1915

J. C. Leyendecker
MAY 22, 1915

Penrhyn Stanlaws
MAY 29, 1915

Sarah Stilwell-Weber
JUNE 5, 1915

J. C. Leyendecker
JUNE 12, 1915

Harrison Fisher
JUNE 19, 1915

William Haskell Coffin
JUNE 26, 1915

J. C. Leyendecker
JULY 3, 1915

Martin Justice
JULY 10, 1915

Frank H. Desch
JULY 17, 1915

J. C. Leyendecker
JULY 24, 1915

William Haskell Coffin
JULY 31, 1915

J. C. Leyendecker
AUGUST 7, 1915

Sarah Stilwell-Weber
AUGUST 14, 1915

Z. P. Nikolaki
AUGUST 28, 1915

Sarah Stilwell-Weber
SEPTEMBER 4, 1915

Leslie Thrasher
SEPTEMBER 11, 1915

Charles Livingston Bull
SEPTEMBER 18, 1915

Sarah Stilwell-Weber
SEPTEMBER 25, 1915

Tony Sarg
OCTOBER 2, 1915

Penrhyn Stanlaws
OCTOBER 9, 1915

Leslie Thrasher
OCTOBER 16, 1915

Sarah Stilwell-Weber
OCTOBER 23, 1915

Frederick Duncan
OCTOBER 30, 1915

Charles A. MacLellan
NOVEMBER 6, 1915

Tony Sarg
NOVEMBER 13, 1915

J. C. Leyendecker
NOVEMBER 20, 1915

Z. P. Nikolaki
NOVEMBER 27, 1915

Leslie Thrasher
DECEMBER 4, 1915

J. C. Leyendecker
DECEMBER 11, 1915

Sarah Stilwell-Weber
DECEMBER 18, 1915

J. C. Leyendecker
DECEMBER 25, 1915

J. C. Leyendecker
JANUARY 1, 1916

N. P. Zarokilli
JANUARY 8, 1916

Watson Barratt
JANUARY 15, 1916

Tony Sarg
JANUARY 22, 1916

Sarah Stilwell-Weber
JANUARY 29, 1916

.William Haskell Coffin
FEBRUARY 5, 1916

Charles Livingston Bull
FEBRUARY 12, 1916

Philip Boileau
FEBRUARY 19, 1916

Charles A. MacLellan
FEBRUARY 26, 1916

Sarah Stilwell-Weber
MARCH 4, 1916

J. C. Leyendecker
MARCH 11, 1916

Charles A. MacLellan
MARCH 18, 1916

Clarence F. Underwood
MARCH 25, 1916

Charles Livingston Bull
APRIL 1, 1916

Will Grefe
APRIL 8, 1916

J. C. Leyendecker
APRIL 15, 1916

J. C. Leyendecker
APRIL 22, 1916

Philip Boileau
APRIL 29, 1916

J. C. Leyendecker
MAY 6, 1916

Neysa McMein
MAY 13, 1916

Norman Rockwell
MAY 20, 1916

L. Mayer
MAY 27, 1916

Norman Rockwell
JUNE 3, 1916

Harry Fisk
JUNE 10, 1916

J. C. Leyendecker
JUNE 17, 1916

Clarence F. Underwood
JUNE 24, 1916

J. C. Leyendecker
JULY 1, 1916

Neysa McMein
JULY 8, 1916

Charles A. MacLellan
JULY 15, 1916

Neysa McMein
JULY 22, 1916

Sarah Stilwell-Weber
JULY 29, 1916

Norman Rockwell
AUGUST 5, 1916

Sarah Stilwell-Weber
AUGUST 12, 1916

Clarence F. Underwood
AUGUST 19, 1916

J. C. Leyendecker
AUGUST 26, 1916

N. P. Zarokilli
SEPTEMBER 2, 1916

Cushman Parker
SEPTEMBER 9, 1916

Norman Rockwell
SEPTEMBER 16, 1916

Francis Miller
SEPTEMBER 23, 1916

J. C. Leyendecker
SEPTEMBER 30, 1916

Neysa McMein
OCTOBER 7, 1916

Norman Rockwell
OCTOBER 14, 1916

Sarah Stilwell-Weber
OCTOBER 21, 1916

L. G. Hemsteger
OCTOBER 28, 1916

J. C. Leyendecker
NOVEMBER 4, 1916

Neysa McMein
NOVEMBER 11, 1916

Charles Livingston Bull
NOVEMBER 18, 1916

C. Warde Traver
NOVEMBER 25, 1916

J. C. Leyendecker
DECEMBER 2, 1916

Norman Rockwell
DECEMBER 9, 1916

J. C. Leyendecker
DECEMBER 23, 1916

J. C. Leyendecker
DECEMBER 30, 1916

Philip Boileau
JANUARY 6, 1917

Norman Rockwell
JANUARY 13, 1917

Emil Fuchs
JANUARY 20, 1917

Charles A. MacLellan
JANUARY 27, 1917

Philip Boileau
FEBRUARY 3, 1917

Sarah Stilwell-Weber
FEBRUARY 10, 1917

Neysa McMein
FEBRUARY 17, 1917

Robert Robinson
FEBRUARY 24, 1917

Sarah Stilwell-Weber
MARCH 3, 1917

J. C. Leyendecker
MARCH 10, 1917

Neysa McMein
MARCH 17, 1917

Clarence F. Underwood
MARCH 24, 1917

E. L. Crompton
MARCH 31, 1917

J. C. Leyendecker
APRIL 7, 1917

Neysa McMein
APRIL 14, 1917

Sarah Stilwell-Weber
APRIL 28, 1917

Walter H. Everett
MAY 5, 1917

Norman Rockwell
MAY 12, 1917

J. C. Leyendecker
MAY 19, 1917

Neysa McMein
MAY 26, 1917

Charles A. MacLellan
JUNE 2, 1917

Henry J. Soulen
JUNE 9, 1917

Neysa McMein
JUNE 23, 1917

J. C. Leyendecker
JUNE 30, 1917

Neysa McMein
JULY 7, 1917

Charles A. MacLellan
JULY 14, 1917

Henry J. Soulen
JULY 21, 1917

N. P. Zarokilli
JULY 28, 1917

Charles A. MacLellan
AUGUST 4, 1917

Neysa McMein
AUGUST 11, 1917

Clarence F. Underwood
AUGUST 18, 1917

Sarah Stilwell-Weber
AUGUST 25, 1917

J. C. Leyendecker
SEPTEMBER 1, 1917

Clarence F. Underwood
SEPTEMBER 8, 1917

Charles A. MacLellan
SEPTEMBER 15, 1917

J. C. Leyendecker
SEPTEMBER 22, 1917

Neysa McMein
SEPTEMBER 29, 1917

J. C. Leyendecker
OCTOBER 6, 1917

William Haskell Coffin
OCTOBER 13, 1917

Robert Robinson
OCTOBER 20, 1917

Norman Rockwell
OCTOBER 27, 1917

Charles A. MacLellan
NOVEMBER 3, 1917

J. C. Leyendecker
NOVEMBER 10, 1917

J. C. Leyendecker
NOVEMBER 24, 1917

Clarence F. Underwood
DECEMBER 1, 1917

J. C. Leyendecker
DECEMBER 8, 1917

Neysa McMein
DECEMBER 15, 1917

J. C. Leyendecker
DECEMBER 22, 1917

J. C. Leyendecker
DECEMBER 29, 1917

John F. Sheridan
JANUARY 5, 1918

Harold Brett
JANUARY 12, 1918

Neysa McMein
JANUARY 19, 1918

Norman Rockwell
JANUARY 26, 1918

Clarence F. Underwood
FEBRUARY 2, 1918

Robert Robinson
FEBRUARY 9, 1918

J. C. Leyendecker
FEBRUARY 16, 1918

Francis Miller
FEBRUARY 23, 1918

Neysa McMein
MARCH 9, 1918

Charles Livingston Bull
MARCH 16, 1918

J. C. Leyendecker
MARCH 23, 1918

J. C. Leyendecker
MARCH 30, 1918

Sarah Stilwell-Weber
APRIL 6, 1918

Clark Fay
APRIL 13, 1918

Neysa McMein
APRIL 20, 1918

Sarah Stilwell-Weber
APRIL 27, 1918

Neysa McMein
MAY 4, 1918

Julian De Miskey
MAY 11, 1918

Norman Rockwell
MAY 18, 1918

Neysa McMein
MAY 25, 1918

J. C. Leyendecker
JUNE 1, 1918

Clarence F. Underwood
JUNE 8, 1918

Charles A. MacLellan
JUNE 15, 1918

Neysa McMein
JUNE 22, 1918

J. C. Leyendecker
JUNE 29, 1918

J. C. Leyendecker
JULY 6, 1918

Sarah Stilwell-Weber
JULY 13, 1918

Charles A. MacLellan
JULY 20, 1918

J. C. Leyendecker
JULY 27, 1918

J. Knowles Hare
AUGUST 3, 1918

Norman Rockwell
AUGUST 10, 1918

J. C. Leyendecker
AUGUST 17, 1918

Sarah Stilwell-Weber
AUGUST 24, 1918

Neysa McMein
AUGUST 31, 1918

N. P. Zarokilli
SEPTEMBER 14, 1918

Norman Rockwell
SEPTEMBER 21, 1918

Neysa McMein
SEPTEMBER 28, 1918

Sarah Stilwell-Weber
OCTOBER 5, 1918

Robert Robinson
OCTOBER 12, 1918

William Shewell Ellis
OCTOBER 19, 1918

J. C. Leyendecker
OCTOBER 26, 1918

Sarah Stilwell-Weber
NOVEMBER 2, 1918

J. Knowles Hare
NOVEMBER 9, 1918

J. Knowles Hare
NOVEMBER 16, 1918

Charles Livingston Bull
NOVEMBER 23, 1918

J. C. Leyendecker
NOVEMBER 30, 1918

J. C. Leyendecker
DECEMBER 7, 1918

Katharine Richardson Wireman
DECEMBER 14, 1918

J. C. Leyendecker
DECEMBER 21, 1918

William Shewell Ellis
JANUARY 4, 1919

J. Knowles Hare
JANUARY 11, 1919

Norman Rockwell
JANUARY 18, 1919

Sarah Stilwell-Weber
JANUARY 25, 1919

J. Knowles Hare
FEBRUARY 1, 1919

N. P. Zarokilli
FEBRUARY 15, 1919

Norman Rockwell
FEBRUARY 22, 1919

Sarah Stilwell-Weber
MARCH 8, 1919

Neysa McMein
MARCH 15, 1919

Norman Rockwell
MARCH 22, 1919

William Shewell Ellis
MARCH 29, 1919

J. C. Leyendecker
APRIL 5, 1919

William Shewell Ellis
APRIL 12, 1919

J. C. Leyendecker
APRIL 19, 1919

Norman Rockwell
APRIL 26, 1919

Neysa McMein
MAY 3, 1919

J. C. Leyendecker
MAY 10, 1919

J. Knowles Hare
MAY 17, 1919

83

Harold Brett
MAY 24, 1919

J. C. Leyendecker
MAY 31, 1919

Neysa McMein
JUNE 7, 1919

Norman Rockwell
JUNE 14, 1919

L. Mayer
JUNE 21, 1919

Norman Rockwell
JUNE 28, 1919

J. C. Leyendecker
JULY 5, 1919

Sarah Stilwell-Weber
JULY 12, 1919

Neysa McMein
JULY 19, 1919

Charles Livingston Bull
JULY 26, 1919

Neysa McMein
AUGUST 2, 1919

Norman Rockwell
AUGUST 9, 1919

James E. Abbe
AUGUST 16, 1919

J. C. Leyendecker
AUGUST 23, 1919

J. Knowles Hare
AUGUST 30, 1919

Norman Rockwell
SEPTEMBER 6, 1919

Clarence F. Underwood
SEPTEMBER 13, 1919

Norman Rockwell
SEPTEMBER 20, 1919

N. P. Zarokilli
SEPTEMBER 27, 1919

Norman Rockwell
OCTOBER 4, 1919

Neysa McMein
OCTOBER 11, 1919

Cushman Parker
OCTOBER 18, 1919

Neysa McMein
OCTOBER 25, 1919

J. C. Leyendecker
NOVEMBER 1, 1919

Anita Parkhurst
NOVEMBER 8, 1919

Sarah Stilwell-Weber
NOVEMBER 15, 1919

Helen Thurlow
NOVEMBER 22, 1919

J. C. Leyendecker
NOVEMBER 29, 1919

Neysa McMein
DECEMBER 6, 1919

Neysa McMein
DECEMBER 13, 1919

Norman Rockwell
DECEMBER 20, 1919

J. C. Leyendecker
DECEMBER 27, 1919

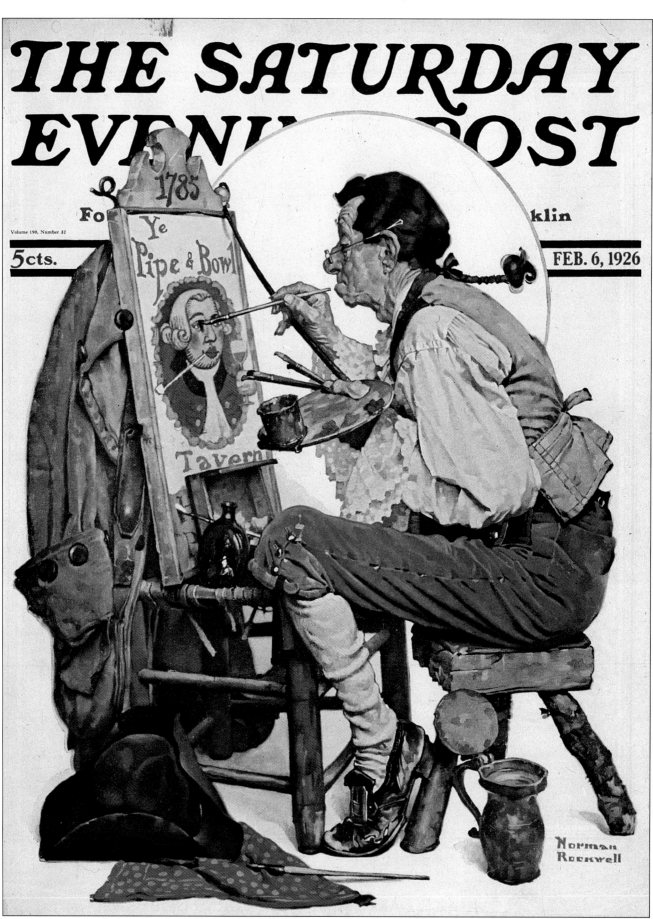

Norman Rockwell
FEBRUARY 6, 1926

CHAPTER 3

THE TWENTIES

The twenties were the heyday of the *Post*. Readers were treated to the best in popular fiction, with short stories by F. Scott Fitzgerald, Joseph Hergesheimer, P. G. Wodehouse, Ben Ames Williams, Earl Derr Biggers, and J. P. Marquand. Long-familiar *Post* writers like Mary Roberts Rinehart, Arthur Train, and Peter B. Kyne continued to publish stories about favorite characters: Tish, Mr. Tutt, and Cappy Ricks. In 1927, the magazine printed William Hazlett Upson's first story about Alexander W. Botts, the unforgettable salesman for Earthworm Tractors. As in the past, nonfiction covered business and politics, but now the *Post* entertained readers with celebrity memoirs as well. During this decade a flood of life stories appeared: of Jim Corbet, Fannie Brice, Luther Burbank, Eddie Cantor, Harold Lloyd, David Sarnoff, Amos Alonzo Stagg, John Philip Sousa, and, with some considerable prettying up, Benito Mussolini.

Post covers during these years featured the work of more than sixty artists. Most of these artists, however, made few appearances on the cover, forty of them only once or twice. As in the preceding decade, the cover of the *Post* was dominated by the work of J. C. Leyendecker, and now by that of Norman Rockwell as well; together they were responsible for one third of all the covers during the 1920s.

Like the rest of America, the *Post* boomed in the twenties. Advertising increased to the point where it made up as much as sixty percent of each issue and, supported by the amount of advertising, the size of the weekly issue often exceeded two hundred pages and carried as many as twenty articles, stories, and installments of serialized novels. Revenues soared; in 1927 the *Post* grossed more than $50 million in advertising. By the end of the decade, weekly circulation had reached 2,865,996.

The prosperity that fueled the leap in advertising and brought *Post* readers huge weekly issues filled with the best in popular writing also made its mark on the cover art. For nearly three decades, *Post* covers had been produced in red and black, the two-color printing varied by the use of different tones. These covers displayed the fine craftsmanship of both the engravers and the printers. By 1926 technological advances had made it possible to achieve the same high quality with four-color printing, and that year the *Post* moved to four-color covers. As the Curtis Company put it in a 1927 promotional publication, *A Short History of* The Saturday Evening Post, "*An American*

Institution in Three Centuries," "In 1926 presses were perfected which solved the triple problem of printing in four colors with a high press output and beautiful reproduction."*

The first four-color cover appeared on February 6, 1926, and the honors went to Norman Rockwell (page 86). In a nod toward Ben Franklin, long claimed as the *Post*'s own founding father, and in a humorous echo of the colonial billboard covers from the first decade, Rockwell made the first four-color cover both a tribute to the past and an opportunity for his own distinctive humor. A somewhat comic, and far from dignified, man in colonial deshabille paints his own billboard, in this case a sign for a tavern that is replacing George III with George Washington.

Whether it was produced in two or four colors, Rockwell's work during these years flowered. Dozens of his covers from this period have outlived their one-week existence on the cover of the *Post* to become part of the heritage of American illustration. Rockwell's forte remained the implied narrative painting, but his range expanded to include other subjects and other moods. His Christmas covers, for example, frequently presented a nineteenth-century world: coaches and coachmen, Victorian musicians and dancers. The romance of the Middle Ages absorbed him as well; sometimes a boy or a middle-aged man in contemporary dress dozes over a book of chivalry, their dreams representing medieval scenes (November 10, 1923; February 16, 1929). Occasionally, Rockwell drew a heroic cover, most memorably in "Pioneer," with the strong face of a pilot facing the viewer, and a sailing ship and a covered

*Frederick S. Bigelow, *A Short History of* The Saturday Evening Post, "*An American Institution in Three Centuries*" ([Philadelphia]: Curtis Company, 1927), p. 34.

wagon in the background (July 23, 1927; bottom left, page 94).

But Rockwell's most frequent subject was boyhood, and the covers that featured boys always told a story. The July 9, 1921, cover shows a boy dressed for a photograph, his head in the metal holder used to keep the sitter immobile; on his knee the miserable boy holds a howling baby, entirely unrestrained despite the occasion. A year later Rockwell painted a picture of longing: through the window of a schoolhouse we see a boy stare out at his faithful dog (June 10, 1922). In a cover the following year, the boy is released; school is out and a joyous boy, shed of his shoes, does handstands (June 23, 1923; top left, page 95).

Rockwell's boys are most often seen with their dogs. The March 10, 1923, cover shows a boy giving a spoonful of medicine to his sick dog. Another, at the end of the decade, presents a ragged boy and his mutt; the boy reaches out his hand to pet an elegant collie, surrounded by fancy luggage and complete with his own luggage tag (September 28, 1929; bottom right, page 95). Sometimes the boy is shown at the edge of manhood. On September 27, 1924, a rural young man off to the city to make good hugs his dog good-bye.

Whether in imitation of Rockwell or simply because boy-and-dog was too good a subject to pass up, other cover artists exploited this theme. Alan Foster, who did more than twenty covers during these years, tried his hand at painting the end of the school day; his cover for September 14, 1929, simply shows four dogs waiting patiently by a country school. E. M. Jackson, who painted more than thirty *Post* covers during the twenties, rendered a boy smuggling Christmas dinner to his under-the-table dog (December 15, 1923). Jackson also drew the most sentimental of the boy and

dog covers. In one a boy is shown beside the grave of his dog, Tige (August 16, 1924).

Rockwell sometimes painted girls, though most of these covers brought a girl together with an older, and sometimes a very old, man. One example presented a portly old fellow scraping away on a cello while a little girl, presumably his granddaughter, holds her skirts and dances (February 3, 1923). In a particularly delightful cover, for May 3, 1924, a dour old rural storekeeper tries on a flowered hat for his customer, a small girl who gazes solemnly at him (top left, page 94). A girl appears alone in a 1929 cover, demurely covering her eyes as she passes the sign for the local swimming hole, with the discarded clothes of the swimming boys much in evidence (June 15).

In the twenties, as in the preceding decade, oldsters, and especially older men, were frequent subjects for comic narrative covers. Rockwell trained his eye on middle-aged and older men with remarkable results. An elderly clerk sorts the mail, stopping to read a postcard addressed to Miss Daisy Dell (February 18, 1922). A balding man struggles to thread a needle to darn the hole in his sock, while his cat, ignored, rubs up against his leg (April 8, 1922). A rural station master, next to a trunk marked "RUSH!" sleeps through a hot afternoon (August 29, 1925; top right, page 94). An absent-minded professor, next to an empty shopping basket with a note tied to it, loses himself in a book at an outdoor stall (August 14, 1926).

A number of Rockwell's covers from this period, using a variety of characters, express longing for what once was or what is not; in some cases a boy strives to realize his dreams. In one, a skinny kid works out with barbells (April 29, 1922; bottom right, page 94); in another, a young man, overseen by a photograph of Lincoln, studies a law book, a barrel as his desk (April 29, 1922; February 19, 1927). Old men, too, have desires, sometimes attainable and at other times beyond their reach. For the November 2, 1929, cover, Rockwell painted an old violinist; he stands in the street, carrying his violin case and staring at a display of a saxophone and modern sheet music. A few years earlier, Rockwell had painted another old violinist; in this case, he is the concert master and he listens with distinct disapprobation to the soulful playing of a dandified young virtuoso soloist (April 28, 1923). Longing returns in a particularly striking example for June 14, 1924; here, a peglegged pirate faces the viewer, and in the background is his old cottage home, presumably his memory of a happier time.

One other character type engaged Rockwell's imagination from time to time: the hobo or tramp. For October 18, 1924, he painted a hobo, his dog beside him, roasting a frankfurter over a fire. The next year the tramp became a nineteenth-century gent, in seedy finery; at his ease in a comfortable chair, he cautiously gropes with his stick to reach a cigar butt on the floor (July 11, 1925). Later in the decade Rockwell painted the clichéd image of the tramp stealing a pie, but in his hands it turns into a spirited moment as the family dog latches on to the tramp's pants (August 18, 1928; top right, page 95). The tramp appeared in the work of other artists as well. On January 23, 1926, Leyendecker showed him eyeing an ax and a pile of unsplit wood, in his pocket a brochure advertising Palm Beach. In E. F. Wittmack's hands, the tramp appears on the road, thumbing a ride to Florida; his pockets are filled with come-ons for land sales (October 24, 1925).

J. C. Leyendecker's work continued to vary in subject and style throughout the twenties. Once again, the range in his talent is dramatically illustrated by the difference between his New Year's and his Christmas covers. For the New Year, of course, the Leyendecker baby continued to make his— or her—appearance, one year laboring with a pickax and hard hat, another an unhappy taxpayer, preparing to chop the roll of income tax in half with an ax (January 1, 1921; January 2, 1926). But for Christmas, Leyendecker was much more sentimental in his subject and much more elaborate in his drawing. A frequent subject was mother and child. Early in the decade he painted a mother listening to her son's prayers; a particular Christmas touch is shown in her clothing: the jacket she wears is a short-sleeved version of Santa's coat (December 24, 1921). On the cover for December 23, 1922, he painted a lovely woman and a sleeping baby, with the suggestion of halos around both heads. By the end of the decade he had turned directly to the Madonna and Child, painted in a Gothic style (December 22, 1928).

Leyendecker also continued to paint the Thanksgiving cover. In 1921 and 1922 his baby made special appearances. For the earlier year, he wore a chef's hat and an executioner's mask and waited, his cleaver on a block; for the second, still with his chef's hat, he dragged an enormous and reluctant turkey by a rope around its neck (November 26, 1921; November 25, 1922). Sometimes he turned to history, in one instance painting a cover with an Indian and a Pilgrim; the Indian has a turkey and the Pilgrim offers beads (December 1, 1923). The Pilgrim reappeared on November 29, 1924, carrying a Bible and a musket, and again on November 24, 1928, joined by a football player.

Leyendecker painted story covers, too, sometimes with particular finesse, as in two covers from 1922. In one, a handsome motorcycle cop has stopped a small wooden car, pretending to ticket the little boy driver. Like the stereotypical male motorist, the small boy stares back with an innocent "Who, me?" expression. But in the backseat, the little girl who accompanies him clutches his clothes and weeps (June 24). The second cover flirts with sentimentality. It shows a poor elderly man with a collie puppy under each arm and a basket with a For Sale sign; beside him is the collie mother, and the two eye each other sadly (October 14, 1922).

Over the decade, a handful of other artists contributed a dozen or more covers. Some of them, including Haskell Coffin, Charles A. MacLellan, Neysa McMein, and Penrhyn Stanlaws, provided the *Post* with pictures of beautiful women, continuing that long tradition for the magazine. Coffin and McMein simply painted women, but Stanlaws occasionally and MacLellan nearly always drew their women in scenes that suggested action or, on rare occasions, a story. MacLellan, for example, provided his models with props such as a college textbook (January 27, 1923), a golf club—as well as a divot to prove she couldn't do it right (September 22, 1923; top right, page 93), or a pair of ice skates (January 26, 1924). His women failed not only at golf; one carried a shotgun but stopped to feed a squirrel, while another, driving a car, has been stopped for speeding (November 3, 1923; March 15, 1924). Stanlaws varied his simple, but lovely, portraits by painting one woman deep in snow, making a snowball (February 18, 1928). For the June 9, 1928, cover he, too, showed the futility of women golfers; in his case, it's the golf ball that's been damaged (bottom right, page 93).

Ellen Pyle painted her first *Post* cover in 1923. At first she, too, painted women and, sometimes, girls or babies, but by the end of the decade she was trying more complicated covers. For June 11, 1927, she painted two college graduates; to a modern eye, her conception is, to say the least, odd: the man wears a cap and gown, but the woman sports a pink dress. The next year she did a cover that combined two reliable themes, the poor family and the circus. Here, a mother and her three children watch a circus parade; the free parade is all they can afford to see (August 25, 1928).

Boys, Rockwell's favorite subject, were also the primary subjects for several other artists. Alan Foster contributed covers with boys playing musical instruments or playing baseball. In the latter case (May 28, 1927), one team is uniformed and the other is not; a uniformed baseman stares at a scruffy base runner: will he steal? Foster did some college men, too; on the November 14, 1925, cover a college man holds a letter from his dad, but it is the envelope that holds his attention. He searches it once again for a check.

Eugene Iverd also painted boys, particularly at play. In one cover boys are on their way to play baseball; in another they are engaged in an enormous snowball fight; and in two instances they are out in iceboats (April 17, 1926; January 15, 1927; February 4, 1928; January 19, 1929). E. M. Jackson's boys are sometimes sentimental, as in the May 23, 1925, cover showing a boy, a broken piggy bank, a single penny, and a passing circus parade. Other examples provide comic interaction between boys and objects. As a boy stares wide-eyed at his geography book, the schoolroom globe stares back at him (September 29, 1923). Another boy plays blissfully at the harp, unaware that the figurehead on the harp has stuck her fingers in her offended ears (April 4, 1925).

Leslie Thrasher and Lawrence Toney each did a few covers during these years. In both cases, their subject matter seems deeply influenced by Rockwell. Toney, for example, painted the May 15, 1926, cover, with a little girl excluded from a shack hung with signs announcing it as the private haunt of a boys' club. The March 17, 1928, cover took the party line as its subject: as two women hold a telephone conversation, four others listen in. Thrasher, like Rockwell, painted a boy intent on developing his muscles; in this case, the boy sports a black eye (June 9, 1923). There is a Rockwell feel, as well, in his February 24, 1923, cover illustration of a little man earnestly reading *The Lives of the Great.*

Despite the various styles of the many artists who painted them, the covers of the *Saturday Evening Post* in the twenties have a consistently "modern" look, particularly after the adoption of four-color production. Formerly, cover art for the *Post*, like other illustrations of the period, had been characterized by an emphasis on line. Now, a more painterly, colorist style dominated, enhanced by the use of four-color printing.

But the appearance of the covers was often more modern than the subject matter. It was not, certainly, that the cover artists for the *Post* avoided contemporary subjects; any number of covers dealt with up-to-date material. There were covers about college life, primarily football games, and about the idolization of movie stars. There were covers about Florida, newly discovered as a vacation site and a real estate bonanza. There were dozens of covers of beautiful women, all women of the twenties, engaged in modern activities, more active and less languid, than the beauties of earlier covers. And

there were covers about sports, often told through the experiences of young boys, and particularly about the new craze for golf, with women golfers, as we have seen, flubbing the game. Golf inspired a few particularly witty covers; Walter Beach Humphrey painted one that showed the boss returning to his office to find the office boy trying out his golf clubs (October 20, 1923; bottom left, page 93). In Lawrence Toney's gem we see only the golfer and his caddie; both stand amazed (September 11, 1926; top left, page 93).

But despite these instances of the modern, the overriding experience represented on the covers of the *Post* is one of escape. Sometimes the artist retreats into the past: the Middle Ages, Victorian England, colonial America. More often a more subtle form of escape is presented, through nostalgia for an irrecoverable American past, the past of boyhood or a fast-disappearing rural America. As with the other facets of the *Post* covers at this time, it is Rockwell and Leyendecker who most clearly figure in their work this subtle escape from the present. Two covers are exemplary. For August 3, 1929, Rockwell painted a man in a business suit who has taken over the pole and the line and the bait of a boy out fishing; the boy simply looks on (bottom left, page 95). Leyendecker, in a 1927 cover, is more direct; for Thanksgiving that year he drew an old man dozing and showed us his dream: he dreams of himself as a small boy whose beautiful young mother carries the turkey to the table (November 26).

Lawrence Toney
SEPTEMBER 11, 1926

Charles A. MacLellan
SEPTEMBER 22, 1923

Walter Beach Humphrey
OCTOBER 20, 1923

Penrhyn Stanlaws
JUNE 9, 1928

Norman Rockwell
MAY 3, 1924

Norman Rockwell
AUGUST 29, 1925

Norman Rockwell
JULY 23, 1927

Norman Rockwell
APRIL 29, 1922

Norman Rockwell
JUNE 23, 1923

Norman Rockwell
AUGUST 18, 1928

Norman Rockwell
AUGUST 3, 1929

Norman Rockwell
SEPTEMBER 28, 1929

J. C. Leyendecker
JANUARY 3, 1920

J. Knowles Hare
JANUARY 10, 1920

Norman Rockwell
JANUARY 17, 1920

J. C. Leyendecker
JANUARY 24, 1920

Neysa McMein
JANUARY 31, 1920

Norman Rockwell
FEBRUARY 7, 1920

Clarence F. Underwood
FEBRUARY 14, 1920

Sarah Stilwell-Weber
FEBRUARY 21, 1920

Angus MacDonall
FEBRUARY 28, 1920

Neysa McMein
MARCH 6, 1920

J. C. Leyendecker
MARCH 13, 1920

C. Warde Traver
MARCH 20, 1920

Norman Rockwell
MARCH 27, 1920

J. C. Leyendecker
APRIL 3, 1920

Neysa McMein
APRIL 10, 1920

Angus MacDonall
APRIL 17, 1920

Neysa McMein
APRIL 24, 1920

NORMAN ROCKWELL
MAY 1, 1920

J. Knowles Hare
MAY 8, 1920

Norman Rockwell
MAY 15, 1920

Anita Parkhurst
MAY 22, 1920

Neysa McMein
MAY 29, 1920

J. C. Leyendecker
JUNE 5, 1920

Anita Parkhurst
JUNE 12, 1920

Norman Rockwell
JUNE 19, 1920

Clarence F. Underwood
JUNE 26, 1920

J. C. Leyendecker
JULY 3, 1920

Anita Parkhurst
JULY 10, 1920

Sarah Stilwell Weber
JULY 17, 1920

Frank H. Desch
JULY 24, 1920

Norman Rockwell
JULY 31, 1920

Neysa McMein
AUGUST 7, 1920

97

Alfred E. Orr
AUGUST 14, 1920

Arthur Garratt
AUGUST 21, 1920

Norman Rockwell
AUGUST 28, 1920

Coles Phillips
SEPTEMBER 4, 1920

Neysa McMein
SEPTEMBER 11, 1920

J. C. Leyendecker
SEPTEMBER 18, 1920

Alfred E. Orr
SEPTEMBER 25, 1920

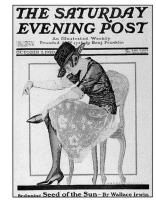

Coles Phillips
OCTOBER 2, 1920

Norman Rockwell
OCTOBER 9, 1920

Alfred E. Orr
OCTOBER 16, 1920

Norman Rockwell
OCTOBER 23, 1920

J. C. Leyendecker
OCTOBER 30, 1920

Coles Phillips
NOVEMBER 6, 1920

Neysa McMein
NOVEMBER 13, 1920

Leslie Thrasher
NOVEMBER 20, 1920

J. C. Leyendecker
NOVEMBER 27, 1920

Norman Rockwell
DECEMBER 4, 1920

Alfredo Galli
DECEMBER 11, 1920

Ruth Eastman
DECEMBER 18, 1920

J. C. Leyendecker
DECEMBER 25, 1920

J. C. Leyendecker
JANUARY 1, 1921

Neysa McMein
JANUARY 8, 1921

E. M. Jackson
JANUARY 15, 1921

Coles Phillips
JANUARY 22, 1921

Norman Rockwell
JANUARY 29, 1921

Neysa McMein
FEBRUARY 5, 1921

Frederic Stanley
FEBRUARY 12, 1921

Clarence Underwood
FEBRUARY 19, 1921

F. Earl Christy
FEBRUARY 26, 1921

Alfred E. Orr
MARCH 5, 1921

Norman Rockwell
MARCH 12, 1921

Neysa McMein
MARCH 19, 1921

J. C. Leyendecker
MARCH 26, 1921

Angus MacDonall
APRIL 2, 1921

Anita Parkhurst
APRIL 9, 1921

Neysa McMein
APRIL 16, 1921

Alfred E. Orr
APRIL 23, 1921

Frederic Stanley
APRIL 30, 1921

M. J. Spero
MAY 7, 1921

J. C. Leyendecker
MAY 14, 1921

Neysa McMein
MAY 21, 1921

Sarah Stilwell-Weber
MAY 28, 1921

Norman Rockwell
JUNE 4, 1921

J. C. Leyendecker
JUNE 11, 1921

Neysa McMein
JUNE 18, 1921

Alfred E. Orr
JUNE 25, 1921

J. C. Leyendecker
JULY 2, 1921

Norman Rockwell
JULY 9, 1921

Neysa McMein
JULY 16, 1921

Sarah Stilwell-Weber
JULY 23, 1921

Charles A. MacLellan
JULY 30, 1921

Coles Phillips
AUGUST 6, 1921

Norman Rockwell
AUGUST 13, 1921

Neysa McMein
AUGUST 20, 1921

Katharine Richardson Wireman
AUGUST 27, 1921

J. C. Leyendecker
SEPTEMBER 3, 1921

Paul Stahr
SEPTEMBER 10, 1921

Neysa McMein
SEPTEMBER 17, 1921

J. C. Leyendecker
SEPTEMBER 24, 1921

Norman Rockwell
OCTOBER 1, 1921

Angus MacDonall
OCTOBER 8, 1921

Ronald Anderson
OCTOBER 15, 1921

W. H. D. Koerner
OCTOBER 22, 1921

Frederic Stanley
OCTOBER 29, 1921

Charles Livingston Bull
NOVEMBER 5, 1921

J. Knowles Hare
NOVEMBER 12, 1921

Frederic Stanley
NOVEMBER 19, 1921

J. C. Leyendecker
NOVEMBER 26, 1921

Norman Rockwell
DECEMBER 3, 1921

J. C. Leyendecker
DECEMBER 10, 1921

Neysa McMein
DECEMBER 17, 1921

J. C. Leyendecker
DECEMBER 24, 1921

J. C. Leyendecker
DECEMBER 31, 1921

Angus MacDonall
JANUARY 7, 1922

Norman Rockwell
JANUARY 14, 1922

Ellen Pyle
JANUARY 21, 1922

Clark Fay
JANUARY 28, 1922

Ellen Pyle
FEBRUARY 4, 1922

E. M. Jackson
FEBRUARY 11, 1922

Norman Rockwell
FEBRUARY 18, 1922

Remington Schuyler
FEBRUARY 25, 1922

Angus MacDonall
MARCH 4, 1922

Neysa McMein
MARCH 11, 1922

J. C. Leyendecker
MARCH 18, 1922

Tom Webb
MARCH 25, 1922

W. H. D. Koerner
APRIL 1, 1922

Norman Rockwell
APRIL 8, 1922

J. C. Leyendecker
APRIL 15, 1922

Neysa McMein
APRIL 22, 1922

Ellen Pyle
MAY 6, 1922

Tom Webb
MAY 13, 1922

Norman Rockwell
MAY 20, 1922

Neysa McMein
MAY 27, 1922

F. M. Jackson
JUNE 3, 1922

Norman Rockwell
JUNE 10, 1922

Ellen Pyle
JUNE 17, 1922

J. C. Leyendecker
JUNE 24, 1922

Ellen Pyle
JULY 1, 1922

Neysa McMein
JULY 8, 1922

Coles Phillips
JULY 15, 1922

Paul Stahr
JULY 22, 1922

J. C. Leyendecker
JULY 29, 1922

Paul Bransom
AUGUST 5, 1922

Ellen Pyle
AUGUST 12, 1922

Norman Rockwell
AUGUST 19, 1922

J. C. Leyendecker
AUGUST 26, 1922

Charles A. MacLellan
SEPTEMBER 2, 1922

Norman Rockwell
SEPTEMBER 9, 1922

E. M. Jackson
SEPTEMBER 16, 1922

Coles Phillips
SEPTEMBER 23, 1922

E. M. Jackson
SEPTEMBER 30, 1922

Neysa McMein
OCTOBER 7, 1922

J. C. Leyendecker
OCTOBER 14, 1922

Charles A. MacLellan
OCTOBER 21, 1922

E. M. Jackson
OCTOBER 28, 1922

Norman Rockwell
NOVEMBER 4, 1922

Pearl L. Hill
NOVEMBER 11, 1922

Coles Phillips
NOVEMBER 18, 1922

J. C. Leyendecker
NOVEMBER 25, 1922

Norman Rockwell
DECEMBER 2, 1922

E. M. Jackson
DECEMBER 9, 1922

Neysa McMein
DECEMBER 16, 1922

J. C. Leyendecker
DECEMBER 23, 1922

J. C. Leyendecker
DECEMBER 30, 1922

Ellen Pyle
JANUARY 6, 1923

Walter Beach Humphrey
JANUARY 13, 1923

Alan Foster
JANUARY 20, 1923

Charles A. MacLellan
JANUARY 27, 1923

Norman Rockwell
FEBRUARY 3, 1923

Robert H. Ransley
FEBRUARY 10, 1923

Coles Phillips
FEBRUARY 17, 1923

Leslie Thrasher
FEBRUARY 24, 1923

Neysa McMein
MARCH 3, 1923

Norman Rockwell
MARCH 10, 1923

J. C. Leyendecker
MARCH 17, 1923

Charles A. MacLellan
MARCH 24, 1923

J. C. Leyendecker
MARCH 31, 1923

Rolf Armstrong
APRIL 7, 1923

Pearl L. Hill
APRIL 14, 1923

Reginald F. Bolles
APRIL 21, 1923

Norman Rockwell
APRIL 28, 1923

Neysa McMein
MAY 5, 1923

E. M. Jackson
MAY 12, 1923

Walter Beach Humphrey
MAY 19, 1923

Norman Rockwell
MAY 26, 1923

J. C. Leyendecker
JUNE 2, 1923

Leslie Thrasher
JUNE 9, 1923

Rolf Armstrong
JUNE 16, 1923

J. C. Leyendecker
JUNE 30, 1923

Pearl L. Hill
JULY 7, 1923

Leslie Thrasher
JULY 14, 1923

Walter Beach Humphrey
JULY 21, 1923

E. M. Jackson
JULY 28, 1923

Charles A. MacLellan
AUGUST 4, 1923

Leslie Thrasher
AUGUST 11, 1923

Norman Rockwell
AUGUST 18, 1923

J. C. Leyendecker
AUGUST 25, 1923

Pearl L. Hill
SEPTEMBER 1, 1923

Norman Rockwell
SEPTEMBER 8, 1923

Alan Foster
SEPTEMBER 15, 1923

E. M. Jackson
SEPTEMBER 29, 1923

J. C. Leyendecker
OCTOBER 6, 1923

Joseph Farrelly
OCTOBER 13, 1923

J. C. Leyendecker
OCTOBER 27, 1923

Charles A. MacLellan
NOVEMBER 3, 1923

Norman Rockwell
NOVEMBER 10, 1923

Coles Phillips
NOVEMBER 17, 1923

E. M. Jackson
NOVEMBER 24, 1923

J. C. Leyendecker
DECEMBER 1, 1923

Norman Rockwell
DECEMBER 8, 1923

E. M. Jackson
DECEMBER 15, 1923

J. C. Leyendecker
DECEMBER 22, 1923

J. C. Leyendecker
DECEMBER 29, 1923

Harry Solon
JANUARY 5, 1924

Leslie Thrasher
JANUARY 12, 1924

Guernsey Moore
JANUARY 19, 1924

Charles A. MacLellan
JANUARY 26, 1924

Frederic Stanley
FEBRUARY 2, 1924

Pearl L. Hill
FEBRUARY 9, 1924

J. C. Leyendecker
FEBRUARY 16, 1924

Walter Beach Humphrey
FEBRUARY 23, 1924

Norman Rockwell
MARCH 1, 1924

R. M. Crosby
MARCH 8, 1924

Charles A. MacLellan
MARCH 15, 1924

Charles Livingston Bull
MARCH 22, 1924

Harry Solon
MARCH 29, 1924

Norman Rockwell
APRIL 5, 1924

Frederic Stanley
APRIL 12, 1924

J. C. Leyendecker
APRIL 19, 1924

Neil Hott
APRIL 26, 1924

Robert H. Ransley
MAY 10, 1924

Charles H. Towne
MAY 17, 1924

Penrhyn Stanlaws
MAY 24, 1924

J. F. Kernan
MAY 31, 1924

Norman Rockwell
JUNE 7, 1924

Norman Rockwell
JUNE 14, 1924

Charles A. MacLellan
JUNE 21, 1924

Katharine Richardson Wireman
JUNE 28, 1924

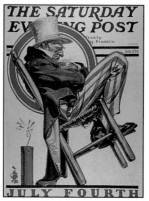

J. C. Leyendecker
JULY 5, 1924

James Calvert Smith
JULY 12, 1924

Norman Rockwell
JULY 19, 1924

Pearl L. Hill
JULY 26, 1924

Frederic Stanley
AUGUST 2, 1924

J. C. Leyendecker
AUGUST 9, 1924

E. M. Jackson
AUGUST 16, 1924

Charles A. MacLellan
AUGUST 23, 1924

Norman Rockwell
AUGUST 30, 1924

Frederic Stanley
SEPTEMBER 6, 1924

Charles A. MacLellan
SEPTEMBER 13, 1924

J. C. Leyendecker
SEPTEMBER 20, 1924

Norman Rockwell
SEPTEMBER 27, 1924

C. W. Anderson
OCTOBER 4, 1924

Alan Foster
OCTOBER 11, 1924

Norman Rockwell
OCTOBER 18, 1924

J. C. Leyendecker
OCTOBER 25, 1924

Pearl L. Hill
NOVEMBER 1, 1924

Norman Rockwell
NOVEMBER 8, 1924

Charles A. MacLellan
NOVEMBER 15, 1924

Charles A. MacLellan
NOVEMBER 22, 1924

J. C. Leyendecker
NOVEMBER 29, 1924

Norman Rockwell
DECEMBER 6, 1924

Charles A. MacLellan
DECEMBER 13, 1924

J. C. Leyendecker
DECEMBER 20, 1924

E. M. Jackson
DECEMBER 27, 1924

J. C. Leyendecker
JANUARY 3, 1925

Arthur Garratt
JANUARY 10, 1925

James Calvert Smith
JANUARY 17, 1925

Tom Webb
JANUARY 24, 1925

Norman Rockwell
JANUARY 31, 1925

Arthur Garratt
FEBRUARY 7, 1925

E. M. Jackson
FEBRUARY 14, 1925

James Calvert Smith
FEBRUARY 21, 1925

Roy Best
FEBRUARY 28, 1925

Paul Stahr
MARCH 7, 1925

Paul Bransom
MARCH 14, 1925

Pearl L. Hill
MARCH 21, 1925

J. C. Leyendecker
MARCH 28, 1925

E. M. Jackson
APRIL 4, 1925

J. C. Leyendecker
APRIL 11, 1925

Norman Rockwell
APRIL 18, 1925

Edmund Davenport
APRIL 25, 1925

Robert C. Kauffmann
MAY 2, 1925

Robert Robinson
MAY 9, 1925

Norman Rockwell
MAY 16, 1925

E. M. Jackson
MAY 23, 1925

Edmund Davenport
MAY 30, 1925

George Brehm
JUNE 6, 1925

Edmund Davenport
JUNE 13, 1925

Harry F. Rudd
JUNE 20, 1925

Norman Rockwell
JUNE 27, 1925

J. C. Leyendecker
JULY 4, 1925

Norman Rockwell
JULY 11, 1925

J. Knowles Hare
JULY 18, 1925

E. M. Jackson
JULY 25, 1925

Charles A. MacLellan
AUGUST 1, 1925

Lawrence Toney
AUGUST 8, 1925

J. Knowles Hare
AUGUST 15, 1925

Alan Foster
AUGUST 22, 1925

George Brehm
SEPTEMBER 5, 1925

Paul Stahr
SEPTEMBER 12, 1925

Norman Rockwell
SEPTEMBER 19, 1925

Charles A. MacLellan
SEPTEMBER 26, 1925

Paul Bransom
OCTOBER 3, 1925

Edgar Franklin Wittmack
OCTOBER 10, 1925

W. Haskell Coffin
OCTOBER 17, 1925

Edgar Franklin Wittmack
OCTOBER 24, 1925

Charles Sheldon
OCTOBER 31, 1925

Frederic Stanley
NOVEMBER 7, 1925

Alan Foster
NOVEMBER 14, 1925

Norman Rockwell
NOVEMBER 21, 1925

J. C. Leyendecker
NOVEMBER 28, 1925

Norman Rockwell
DECEMBER 5, 1925

W. Haskell Coffin
DECEMBER 12, 1925

Neil Hott
DECEMBER 19, 1925

J. C. Leyendecker
DECEMBER 26, 1925

J. C. Leyendecker
JANUARY 2, 1926

Norman Rockwell
JANUARY 9, 1926

Henry J. Soulen
JANUARY 16, 1926

J. C. Leyendecker
JANUARY 23, 1926

Lawrence Toney
JANUARY 30, 1926

Paul Stahr
FEBRUARY 13, 1926

Penrhyn Stanlaws
FEBRUARY 20, 1926

Robert L. Dickey
FEBRUARY 27, 1926

Charles A. MacLellan
MARCH 6, 1926

Eugene Iuard
MARCH 13, 1926

Clarence Underwood
MARCH 20, 1926

Norman Rockwell
MARCH 27, 1926

J. C. Leyendecker
APRIL 3, 1926

Edgar Franklin Wittmack
APRIL 10, 1926

Eugene Iverd
APRIL 17, 1926

Norman Rockwell
APRIL 24, 1926

W. Haskell Coffin
MAY 1, 1926

Edgar Franklin Wittmack
MAY 8, 1926

Lawrence Toney
MAY 15, 1926

Penrhyn Stanlaws
MAY 22, 1926

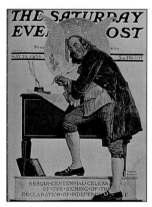

Norman Rockwell
MAY 29, 1926

Alan Foster
JUNE 5, 1926

W. Haskell Coffin
JUNE 12, 1926

Robert L. Dickey
JUNE 19, 1926

Norman Rockwell
JUNE 26, 1926

E. M. Jackson
JULY 3, 1926

Ellen Pyle
JULY 10, 1926

J. C. Leyendecker
JULY 17, 1926

E. M. Jackson
JULY 24, 1926

Robert L. Dickey
JULY 31, 1926

Ellen Pyle
AUGUST 7, 1926

Norman Rockwell
AUGUST 14, 1926

Charles A. MacLellan
AUGUST 21, 1926

Norman Rockwell
AUGUST 28, 1926

Bradshaw Crandall
SEPTEMBER 4, 1926

Paul Bransom
SEPTEMBER 18, 1926

W. Haskell Coffin
SEPTEMBER 25, 1926

Norman Rockwell
OCTOBER 2, 1926

Edgar Franklin Wittmack
OCTOBER 9, 1926

Harrison McCreary
OCTOBER 16, 1926

Bradshaw Crandall
OCTOBER 23, 1926

Edgar Franklin Wittmack
OCTOBER 30, 1926

Edgar Franklin Wittmack
NOVEMBER 6, 1926

Frederic Stanley
NOVEMBER 13, 1926

Alan Foster
NOVEMBER 20, 1926

J. C. Leyendecker
NOVEMBER 27, 1926

Norman Rockwell
DECEMBER 4, 1926

W. Haskell Coffin
DECEMBER 11, 1926

Ellen Pyle
DECEMBER 18, 1926

J. C. Leyendecker
DECEMBER 25, 1926

J. C. Leyendecker
JANUARY 1, 1927

Norman Rockwell
JANUARY 8, 1927

Eugene Iverd
JANUARY 15, 1927

Ellen Pyle
JANUARY 22, 1927

Frederic Stanley
JANUARY 29, 1927

Edna Crompton
FEBRUARY 5, 1927

E. M. Jackson
FEBRUARY 12, 1927

Norman Rockwell
FEBRUARY 19, 1927

W. Haskell Coffin
FEBRUARY 26, 1927

Robert L. Dickey
MARCH 5, 1927

Norman Rockwell
MARCH 12, 1927

W. Haskell Coffin
MARCH 19, 1927

Edgar Franklin Wittmack
MARCH 26, 1927

Henry J. Soulen
APRIL 2, 1927

Frederic Stanley
APRIL 9, 1927

Norman Rockwell
APRIL 16, 1927

E. M. Jackson
APRIL 23, 1927

Frederic Stanley
APRIL 30, 1927

J. C. Leyendecker
MAY 7, 1927

E. M. Jackson
MAY 14, 1927

W. Haskell Coffin
MAY 21, 1927

Alan Foster
MAY 28, 1927

Norman Rockwell
JUNE 4, 1927

Ellen Pyle
JUNE 11, 1927

Penrhyn Stanlaws
JUNE 18, 1927

Eugene Iverd
JUNE 25, 1927

J. C. Leyendecker
JULY 2, 1927

Revere F. Wistehuff
JULY 9, 1927

Alan Foster
JULY 16, 1927

Eugene Iverd
JULY 30, 1927

Ellen Pyle
AUGUST 6, 1927

Norman Rockwell
AUGUST 13, 1927

Bradshaw Crandall
AUGUST 20, 1927

J. C. Leyendecker
AUGUST 27, 1927

George Brehm
SEPTEMBER 3, 1927

Lawrence Toney
SEPTEMBER 10, 1927

J. F. Kernan
SEPTEMBER 17, 1927

Norman Rockwell
SEPTEMBER 24, 1927

Eugene Iverd
OCTOBER 1, 1927

Ellen Pyle
OCTOBER 8, 1927

W. Haskell Coffin
OCTOBER 15, 1927

Norman Rockwell
OCTOBER 22, 1927

Eugene Iverd
OCTOBER 29, 1927

W. Haskell Coffin
NOVEMBER 5, 1927

Alan Foster
NOVEMBER 12, 1927

Bradshaw Crandall
NOVEMBER 19, 1927

J. C. Leyendecker
NOVEMBER 26, 1927

Norman Rockwell
DECEMBER 3, 1927

W. Haskell Coffin
DECEMBER 10, 1927

Alan Foster
DECEMBER 17, 1927

J. C. Leyendecker
DECEMBER 24, 1927

J. C. Leyendecker
DECEMBER 31, 1927

Alan Foster
JANUARY 7, 1928

Henry J. Soulen
JANUARY 14, 1928

Norman Rockwell
JANUARY 21, 1928

Ellen Pyle
JANUARY 28, 1928

Eugene Iverd
FEBRUARY 4, 1928

D. M. Jackson
FEBRUARY 11, 1928

Penrhyn Stanlaws
FEBRUARY 18, 1928

E. M. Jackson
FEBRUARY 25, 1928

Eugene Iverd
MARCH 3, 1928

E. M. Jackson
MARCH 10, 1928

Lawrence Toney
MARCH 17, 1928

Penrhyn Stanlaws
MARCH 24, 1928

Lawrence Toney
MARCH 31, 1928

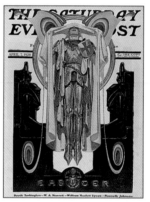

J. C. Leyendecker
APRIL 7, 1928

Norman Rockwell
APRIL 14, 1928

E. M. Jackson
APRIL 21, 1928

W. Haskell Coffin
APRIL 28, 1928

Norman Rockwell
MAY 5, 1928

Edgar Franklin Wittmack
MAY 12, 1928

E. M. Jackson
MAY 19, 1928

Norman Rockwell
MAY 26, 1928

J. C. Leyendecker
JUNE 2, 1928

E. M. Jackson
JUNE 16, 1928

Norman Rockwell
JUNE 23, 1928

J. C. Leyendecker
JUNE 30, 1928

Bradshaw Crandall
JULY 7, 1928

Robert L. Dickey
JULY 14, 1928

Norman Rockwell
JULY 21, 1928

Eugene Iverd
JULY 28, 1928

E. M. Jackson
AUGUST 4, 1928

Lawrence Toney
AUGUST 11, 1928

Ellen Pyle
AUGUST 25, 1928

Alan Foster
SEPTEMBER 1, 1928

J. F. Kernan
SEPTEMBER 8, 1928

Eugene Iverd
SEPTEMBER 15, 1928

Norman Rockwell
SEPTEMBER 22, 1928

Alan Foster
SEPTEMBER 29, 1928

W. H. D. Koerner
OCTOBER 6, 1928

Ellen Pyle
OCTOBER 13, 1928

Alan Foster
OCTOBER 20, 1928

Frederic Stanley
OCTOBER 27, 1928

J. F. Kernan
NOVEMBER 3, 1928

W. Haskell Coffin
NOVEMBER 10, 1928

Eugene Iverd
NOVEMBER 17, 1928

J. C. Leyendecker
NOVEMBER 24, 1928

E. M. Jackson
DECEMBER 1, 1928

Norman Rockwell
DECEMBER 8, 1928

Julio Kilenyi
DECEMBER 15, 1928

J. C. Leyendecker
DECEMBER 22, 1928

J. C. Leyendecker
DECEMBER 29, 1928

E. M. Jackson
JANUARY 5, 1929

Norman Rockwell
JANUARY 12, 1929

Eugene Iverd
JANUARY 19, 1929

W. Haskell Coffin
JANUARY 26, 1929

J. F. Kernan
FEBRUARY 2, 1929

E. M. Jackson
FEBRUARY 9, 1929

Norman Rockwell
FEBRUARY 16, 1929

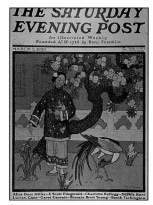

Blanche Greer
FEBRUARY 23, 1929

Henry J. Soulen
MARCH 2, 1929

Norman Rockwell
MARCH 9, 1929

Sam Brown
MARCH 16, 1929

W. Haskell Coffin
MARCH 23, 1929

J. C. Leyendecker
MARCH 30, 1929

Edgar Franklin Wittmack
APRIL 6, 1929

James C. McKell
APRIL 13, 1929

Norman Rockwell
APRIL 20, 1929

Paul Bransom
APRIL 27, 1929

Norman Rockwell
MAY 4, 1929

Penrhyn Stanlaws
MAY 11, 1929

Lawrence Toney
MAY 18, 1929

J. F. Kernan
MAY 25, 1929

Alan Foster
JUNE 1, 1929

J. C. Leyendecker
JUNE 8, 1929

Norman Rockwell
JUNE 15, 1929

E. M. Jackson
JUNE 22, 1929

J. C. Leyendecker
JUNE 29, 1929

Penrhyn Stanlaws
JULY 6, 1929

Norman Rockwell
JULY 13, 1929

E. M. Jackson
JULY 20, 1929

McClelland Barclay
JULY 27, 1929

Alan Foster
AUGUST 10, 1929

Penrhyn Stanlaws
AUGUST 17, 1929

Lawrence Toney
AUGUST 24, 1929

J. F. Kernan
AUGUST 31, 1929

Harrison McCreary
SEPTEMBER 7, 1929

Alan Foster
SEPTEMBER 14, 1929

Henry J. Soulen
SEPTEMBER 21, 1929

J. F. Kernan
OCTOBER 5, 1929

Alan Foster
OCTOBER 12, 1929

J. C. Leyendecker
OCTOBER 19, 1929

E. M. Jackson
OCTOBER 26, 1929

Norman Rockwell
NOVEMBER 2, 1929

Ellen Pyle
NOVEMBER 9, 1929

Alan Foster
NOVEMBER 16, 1929

J. C. Leyendecker
NOVEMBER 23, 1929

John LaGatta
NOVEMBER 30, 1929

Norman Rockwell
DECEMBER 7, 1929

E. M. Jackson
DECEMBER 14, 1929

J. C. Leyendecker
DECEMBER 21, 1929

J. C. Leyendecker
DECEMBER 28, 1929

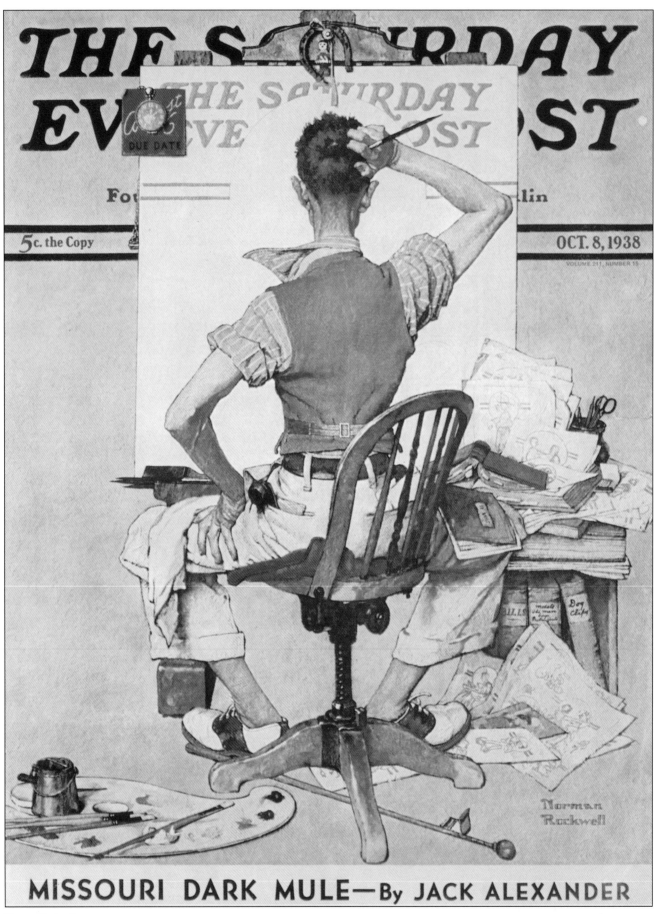

Norman Rockwell
OCTOBER 8, 1938

C H A P T E R 4

THE THIRTIES

The thirties was a decade of change for the *Post*, as it was for America. The magazine, however, suffered not only the economic hardships of the period, but for the first time since editor George Horace Lorimer had brought the *Post* to its dominant position among American periodicals, both editor and magazine found themselves outside the popular mainstream. The election and first administration of Franklin Delano Roosevelt marked a profound change in national values. The *Saturday Evening Post* assumed the opposition role and, during the 1936 election, campaigned both for the restoration of older American values and for the Republican candidate. With the reelection of FDR, Lorimer, his health deteriorating, announced his resignation after thirty-eight years. With the first issue of 1937, the editorship of the *Post* passed to Wesley Stout.

The most visible sign of the changes the thirties brought to the *Post* was its diminished size. The size of the weekly issue was keyed to the number of ads, and as advertising plummeted in the early years of the decade, each issue shrank. In the boom years of the twenties, issues of more than two hundred pages were typical; now, issues of fewer than one hundred pages were not uncommon. The trimmed-down *Post* carried fewer stories, serials, and articles per week, but quality remained high; in fact, with the increased selectivity imposed by smaller issues, the quality of the published material actually improved.

Despite the changes affecting the advertising and editorial aspects of the magazine, the covers of the *Post* remained consistent in both artists and subject matter. As in the past, the work of Leyendecker and Rockwell dominated. Together, their work again made up a third of all the covers during Lorimer's final years as editor. Only a handful of other illustrators—primarily Anton Otto Fischer, Alan Foster, Guy Hoff, Eugene Iverd, E. M. Jackson, J. F. Kernan, John Lagatta, Ellen Pyle, H. J. Soulen, Penrhyn Stanlaws, and E. F. Wittmack—produced six or more covers in as many years. And, with the exception of Fischer and Wittmack, these artists exploited standard themes, including comic narratives typically featuring children or oldsters and portraits of women.

Fischer brought a different subject to the covers of the *Post*; his specialty was ships (page 131). He had a particular fondness for romantic ships, especially the tall sailing vessels of the past. He painted them alone, sailing serenely or battling a storm;

one cover brought the past and present together with a Chinese junk in the foreground and a modern ocean liner in the distance (May 30, 1931; October 31, 1931; December 3, 1932; March 18, 1933). Another specialty was yachts, two racing against each other, or a single graceful yacht veering off as a liner looms close by (September 20, 1930; January 23, 1932).

The subject matter of E. F. Wittmack was also distinctive. Nearly all his covers presented the figure of a man in uniform, in each case the uniform throwing a kind of glamour over the male figure. He painted his models as coast guard officer, Royal Mountie, navy officer (twice), American Legion drummer, and British Guardsman (February 11, 1933; March 25, 1933; February 24 and July 28, 1934; October 7, 1933; October 27, 1934).

Much more typical subject matter was supplied by Guy Hoff, John Lagatta, Ellen Pyle, and Penrhyn Stanlaws, all of whom specialized—in varying styles—in portraits of women. While such portraits were no longer as dominant as they had once been, they remained a frequent and reliable source of subject matter. A considerable number of those artists who sold only one or two cover illustrations to the magazine also painted women, adding to the number produced by more familiar artists. The variety of styles in which women were portrayed ranged from the romantic depictions of Haskell Coffin, who did his last two covers at the beginning of the decade (March 8, 1930; February 28, 1931), to the sleek and sinuous women of Lagatta.

E. M. Jackson painted portraits of women, but he also turned his hand to men and women and to representations of modern relationships. While his covers might be as simple, even as banal, as a picture of a bride and groom (June 6, 1931; page 139,

Anton Otto Fischer
SEPTEMBER 20, 1930

Anton Otto Fischer
MAY 30, 1931

Anton Otto Fischer
DECEMBER 3, 1932

Anton Otto Fischer
OCTOBER 31, 1931

Ellen Pyle
FEBRUARY 22, 1930

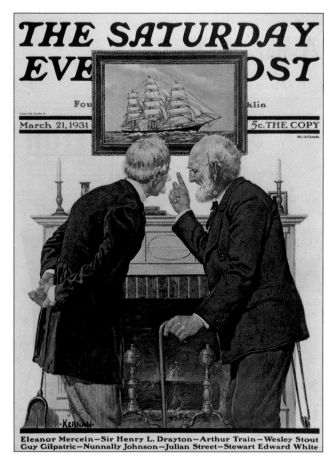

J. F. Kernan
MARCH 21, 1931

J. F. Kernan
NOVEMBER 29, 1930

Ellen Pyle
DECEMBER 13, 1930

top right), he could do more whimsical and evocative work. A particularly nice example of Jackson at his best is the May 10, 1930, cover, which shows a young man and a young woman back to back in barber chairs; she has had her hair bobbed, and the two regard each other's new hairdos (page 139, top left).

Ellen Pyle, who painted more than twenty covers for Lorimer's *Post*, varied her work by also drawing covers that featured children. Sometimes she painted children alone, particularly little girls, one surrounded by chicks, another carefully putting on her socks (May 7, 1932; November 12, 1932). Or she showed children in small groups—for example, a trio on a pier fishing for crabs or two little girls under a large umbrella selling spring flowers in the rain (August 1, 1931; May 5, 1934). But she was equally adept at mixing children and adults. Most often, she paired children with grandmother figures. Among these cover paintings is the one for February 22, 1930 (page 132, top left), with a grandmother holding an earphone to the baby on her lap, another for December 13, 1930 (page 132, bottom right), with a grandmother and a small child all bundled up as they wait for the bus, and a third for October 17, 1931, with a grandmother sewing a button on a boy's coat as a little girl—all dressed for church—waits for them. Pyle's work was clearly valued by Lorimer, for he gave her the Christmas cover in 1932. The cover shows a Madonna and Child motif; Pyle uses simple composition and vibrant color to reflect the radiance of the Madonna (December 17).

Children were also the favored subjects for Alan Foster and Eugene Iverd. Iverd's work generally showed boys engaged in those activities typically thought to belong to the world of the American boy. His boys played baseball, wound up to pitch, tackled each other in football (April 26, 1930; August 18, 1934; November 15, 1930). He showed them stripping off their clothes near a swimming hole or floating in an inner tube, carrying fishing poles and harmonicas or sitting around a fire on the ice (July 21, 1934; August 1, 1936; October 6, 1934; February 21, 1931).

Foster's covers were more explicitly narrative. His boys also play baseball, but he painted them in a fierce quarrel (August 30, 1930). And his boys, like those of Rockwell, are often subjected to the torments adults imposed and the subsequent scorn other children expressed. The September 27, 1930, cover shows one writing over and over on the blackboard, "I was tardy," as a little girl giggles. For March 7, 1931, a boy tugs his little brother uphill on a sled as two other little boys laugh. Foster also juxtaposed the worlds of rich children and poor. The cover for September 19, 1931, features an overdressed rich boy with a hoop; from inside his fenced-off world he watches three "real" boys off to fish. But he could invert the status of rich and poor as well; the cover for the following week stars a poor boy with a wagon full of laundry who looks through a fence at a rich boy's birthday party.

Old folks, particularly old men, had long shared with boys the central role in comic narrative on the covers of the *Post*. In the early years of the thirties, J. F. Kernan did several covers featuring old men, but in his work, comedy gave way to nostalgia. As with Anton Otto Fischer's work, some of Kernan's covers evoke a sense of nostalgia for a past rapidly disappearing under the rush of the modern. In one, two old fellows talk together, recalling their sailing ship days (March 21, 1931; page 132, top right). In another, a man stands on a beach signaling to a boat caught in a storm, but what he imagines is an old three-masted sailing ship

(December 19, 1931). In a third, modern buses and taxis fill the background of the painting, while in the foreground an old coach driver feeds a piece of sugar to his horse (November 29, 1930; page 132, bottom left).

The covers by Leyendecker and Rockwell continued to demonstrate their diversity and range. Leyendecker's work, as always, presented a variety of styles, from contemporary to colonial to medieval. The medieval covers were mainly decorative: a couple with a fleur-de-lis and an English lion, a woman surrounded by flowers, a jester with a lute (July 26, 1930; May 23, 1931; December 26, 1931). Other Leyendecker work had more narrative content. For Thanksgiving in 1930, a boy sick from overeating lies in bed and holds his tongue out for the doctor (November 22). The next year, Thanksgiving preparations have been interrupted: Grandma holds a boy over her knee and spanks him with her shoe, for he has tried to steal her berries and has spilled them on the floor (November 28, 1931; page 135, top right). A particularly complex and ambitious Thanksgiving cover appeared in 1932. In a comic reprise of his great World War I poster featuring the Statue of Liberty handing a sword to a Boy Scout, Leyendecker now painted the United States shield and eagle, but the eagle is a turkey and holds a carving set. The shield bears a pie; on its side bars a boy and a girl kneel, and below them are swags of fruits and vegetables (November 26, 1932; page 135, top left).

Leyendecker's Christmas covers, like much of his work, were marked with captions, and there is a striking move through the decade from the sentimental to the comic. In 1934, he painted "Holy Night," with a nineteenth-century family, the father at the piano, all singing together (December 29, 1934; page 135, bottom left). A year later,

"Silent Night" showed an altogether different vision of family life. Here an infant screams in his high chair while his frazzled parents try to distract him with his Christmas presents, by blowing on his toy horn and beating on his toy drum (December 28, 1935; page 135, bottom right). In 1936, " 'Twas the Night Before Christmas" turns directly to commercialization. A fat woman carries lists and holds the hand of a squalling boy; her husband staggers along loaded down with parcels (December 26).

Meanwhile, Leyendecker's New Year's baby, now a child of the Depression, had become obsessed with the economy. For 1934 he read the stock market tape and found good news for America (December 30, 1933; page 140, top left). In 1935, carrying the budget on his head, he traverses a high wire suspended above pots of red and black ink (January 5, 1935; page 140, top right).

Before the 1936 election, cooperating in the Post's anti-FDR campaign, Leyendecker painted a preelection cover. The Democratic donkey is a small animal with a meager harness and blanket, ridden by a professor. It races futilely to overtake the Republican elephant, a magnificent beast, splendidly caparisoned, its rider a serene businessman in a howdah (October 17, 1936; page 140, bottom left).

Rockwell, too, occasionally touched on the economy. A now-famous 1930 cover showed the backs of four people, whose nineteenth-century dress represents various economic groups, all regarding the stock quotations (January 18, 1930; page 140, bottom right). But much of Rockwell's work from these years ranged widely in its subjects: the movie cowboy having makeup applied; the young husband, lost in the newspaper, and his wife at breakfast; the frustrated mother, her son over her lap, hairbrush in one hand and a book on child

J. C. Leyendecker
NOVEMBER 26, 1932

J. C. Leyendecker
NOVEMBER 28, 1931

J. C. Leyendecker
DECEMBER 29, 1934

J. C. Leyendecker
DECEMBER 28, 1935

psychology in the other, while a broken vase, a broken mirror, a broken lamp ... and a hammer lie on the floor; the young woman and the antiques dealer vigorously haggling; and, on a park bench, a prim little man who peers over his book at a pair of lovers (May 24, 1930, page 138; August 23, 1930—page 139, bottom right; November 25, 1933; May 19, 1934; November 21, 1936—page 139, bottom left).

Once Wesley Stout became editor, he made some changes in the *Post*'s cover art, but the work of Leyendecker and Rockwell remained preeminent. Leyendecker painted his various holiday covers for Stout, and his New Year's baby continued to prognosticate, but now the future was darkened with the prospect of war. In 1938 the baby is shown by a forge, wondering if he will be forging war matériel (January 1). And in the last issue of the decade, he sits on a suitcase, carrying an umbrella but wearing a gas mask (December 30, 1939).

Rockwell, however, maintained his good humor in the later years of the thirties. Even his melancholy covers elicit a smile, whether at the morose ticket agent surrounded by travel posters, the back-to-back dance team, out of work and seated on their trunk, or the dejected Indian at his old mailbox who receives a "See America First" brochure (April 24, 1937; June 12, 1937; April 23, 1938). And some Rockwell work expressed pure euphoria, as with the delighted old maid on her first plane ride (June 4, 1938).

By now, of course, Rockwell was so famous that he could be the subject of his own work; for the October 8, 1938, cover he produced a painting of himself from the back, scratching his head in front of a blank canvas (page 128).

The continuing appearances of Leyendecker and Rockwell on the *Post* cover re-

flect one aspect of Stout's editorship: his desire to maintain the magazine as it had been under Lorimer. But that desire was complicated by an equally strong urge to make his own mark on the *Post*. Those conflicting desires were evident on the covers. If Leyendecker and Rockwell represented the old and familiar *Post*, many of the covers did quite the opposite.

Stout's eagerness to bring change to the cover led him to commission work from an unusually large number of artists new to the magazine. While it had long been *Post* policy to try out new illustrators, in his first three years as editor, Stout introduced thirty new artists, of whom twenty-six did no more than one or two covers. In total, fifty-two covers were done by artists new to the *Post*. Moreover, some artists whose work had been prominent earlier in the decade disappeared from the cover, including Fischer, Iverd, Kernan, Pyle, and Stanlaws. Jackson and Wittmack each did only one cover for Stout.

The most striking, if far from the most successful, change initiated by Stout was the photograph cover. For this work he used Ivan Dmitri, whose four-color photographs were also used inside the magazine, for photojournalism pieces, generally celebrations of picturesque America. Dmitri's work was not particularly distinguished, but he did bring to the cover the kind of dramatic positioning of subject matter that would, in the years to follow, mark much of the cover painting on the *Post* (page 137). His photographs all exaggerate the effects of the close-up or of the shot taken from an awkward angle above or below the subject. The subjects themselves are extremely various. He used modern transportation for some, showing a racing car hood and driver from above or a close-up of a propeller, its housing, and an airplane wing (May 29,

Ivan Dmitri
JULY 16, 1938

Ivan Dmitri
MAY 29, 1937

Ivan Dmitri
NOVEMBER 11, 1939

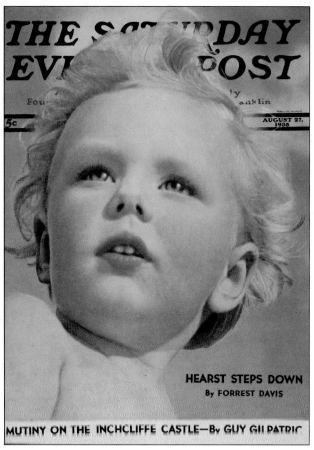

Ivan Dmitri
AUGUST 27, 1938

1937; August 7, 1937). The same close-up technique was used for the May 14, 1938, cover photograph of a dachshund. Shots from below, and close up, were employed for an array of subjects: a lifeguard and his whistle, two West Point cadets, and particularly incongruously, a baby (July 16, 1938; November 11, 1939; August 27, 1938).

Two artists who had done a small amount of work for Lorimer were given a much larger opportunity under Stout. Douglass Crockwell was best known for his work with children, although he handled several different subjects. While some of his covers have charm, he was one of the small army of Rockwell imitators. His boys draw cartoon figures on walls or scowl while having their hair combed or listen in on an older sister's phone conversation (December 11, 1937; July 9, 1938; May 27, 1939). One of his more successful covers appeared on March 20, 1937, with a boy fixing a foxtail to the handle of his bike; in the foreground lie scissors and his mother's mutilated fox fur stole.

Frances Tipton Hunter, too, specialized in children and imitated Rockwell. Her work, which stressed comic narrative, almost always verged on the sentimental. An abashed boy stands before his mother, who holds a union suit up to him for size as an elderly female clerk looks on (February 27, 1937). Another boy is simply uninterested, but his mother shows distress to find that he has outgrown last year's school clothes (September 16, 1939). Boys have fathers, too, as one nervous lad realizes bringing his report card home (March 25, 1939). Perhaps Hunter's most famous cover, much reproduced, shows the heads of five angelic choirboys, several of whom show the results of a prior fist fight (December 10, 1938).

Stout tampered with the covers of the *Post*, but more significant problems faced the magazine's new editor. In the closing years of the decade he was responsible for steering the *Post* through the troubled waters of foreign wars, a stated policy of isolationism, and the growing threat of World War II. When war did come, the *Post*, and its covers, would patriotically enlist.

Norman Rockwell
MAY 24, 1930

E. M. Jackson
MAY 10, 1930

E. M. Jackson
JUNE 6, 1931

Norman Rockwell
NOVEMBER 21, 1936

Norman Rockwell
AUGUST 23, 1930

J. C. Leyendecker
DECEMBER 30, 1933

J. C. Leyendecker
JANUARY 5, 1935

J. C. Leyendecker
OCTOBER 17, 1936

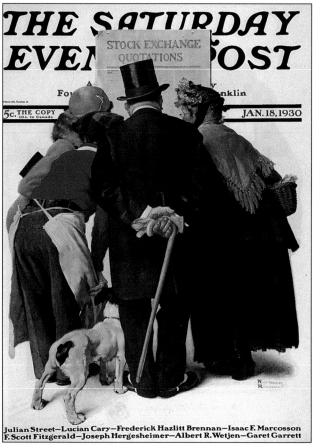

Norman Rockwell
JANUARY 18, 1930

Robert L. Dickey
JANUARY 4, 1930

John LaGatta
JANUARY 11, 1930

J. F. Kernan
JANUARY 25, 1930

McClelland Barclay
FEBRUARY 1, 1930

Alan Foster
FEBRUARY 8, 1930

E. M. Jackson
FEBRUARY 15, 1930

Lawrence Toney
MARCH 1, 1930

W. Haskell Coffin
MARCH 8, 1930

Frederic Stanley
MARCH 15, 1930

Norman Rockwell
MARCH 22, 1930

E. M. Jackson
MARCH 29, 1930

Henry J. Soulen
APRIL 5, 1930

Norman Rockwell
APRIL 12, 1930

J. C. Leyendecker
APRIL 19, 1930

Eugene Iverd
APRIL 26, 1930

J. F. Kernan
MAY 3, 1930

John LaGatta
MAY 17, 1930

Ellen Pyle
MAY 31, 1930

McClelland Barclay
JUNE 7, 1930

E. M. Jackson
JUNE 14, 1930

James C. McKell
JUNE 21, 1930

J. C. Leyendecker
JUNE 28, 1930

John LaGatta
JULY 5, 1930

Lawrence Toney
JULY 12, 1930

Norman Rockwell
JULY 19, 1930

J. C. Leyendecker
JULY 26, 1930

Ellen Pyle
AUGUST 2, 1930

Guy Hoff
AUGUST 9, 1930

Charles Livingston Bull
AUGUST 16, 1930

Alan Foster
AUGUST 30, 1930

J. C. Leyendecker
SEPTEMBER 6, 1930

Norman Rockwell
SEPTEMBER 13, 1930

Alan Foster
SEPTEMBER 27, 1930

Ellen Pyle
OCTOBER 4, 1930

H. W. Tilson
OCTOBER 11, 1930

Sam Brown
OCTOBER 18, 1930

Ellen Pyle
OCTOBER 25, 1930

J. F. Kernan
NOVEMBER 1, 1930

Norman Rockwell
NOVEMBER 8, 1930

Eugene Iverd
NOVEMBER 15, 1930

J. C. Leyendecker
NOVEMBER 22, 1930

Norman Rockwell
DECEMBER 6, 1930

J. C. Leyendecker
DECEMBER 20, 1930

J. C. Leyendecker
DECEMBER 27, 1930

Eugene Iverd
JANUARY 3, 1931

E. M. Jackson
JANUARY 10, 1931

Alan Foster
JANUARY 17, 1931

Guy Hoff
JANUARY 24, 1931

Norman Rockwell
JANUARY 31, 1931

Paul Bransom
FEBRUARY 7, 1931

James C. McKell
FEBRUARY 14, 1931

Eugene Iverd
FEBRUARY 21, 1931

W. Haskell Coffin
FEBRUARY 28, 1931

Alan Foster
MARCH 7, 1931

J. C. Leyendecker
MARCH 14, 1931

Norman Rockwell
MARCH 28, 1931

E. M. Jackson
APRIL 4, 1931

John LaGatta
APRIL 11, 1931

Norman Rockwell
APRIL 18, 1931

E. M. Jackson
APRIL 25, 1931

J. F. Kernan
MAY 2, 1931

Ellen Pyle
MAY 9, 1931

Henry J. Soulen
MAY 16, 1931

J. C. Leyendecker
MAY 23, 1931

Norman Rockwell
JUNE 13, 1931

Ellen Pyle
JUNE 20, 1931

John LaGatta
JUNE 27, 1931

J. C. Leyendecker
JULY 4, 1931

Frederic Stanley
JULY 11, 1931

J. F. Kernan
JULY 18, 1931

Norman Rockwell
JULY 25, 1931

Ellen Pyle
AUGUST 1, 1931

E. M. Jackson
AUGUST 8, 1931

Alan Foster
AUGUST 15, 1931

Alan Foster
AUGUST 22, 1931

Jack Murray
AUGUST 29, 1931

Norman Rockwell
SEPTEMBER 5, 1931

John D. Sheridan
SEPTEMBER 12, 1931

Alan Foster
SEPTEMBER 19, 1931

Alan Foster
SEPTEMBER 26, 1931

J. C. Leyendecker
OCTOBER 3, 1931

Penrhyn Stanlaws
OCTOBER 10, 1931

Ellen Pyle
OCTOBER 17, 1931

W. H. D. Koerner
OCTOBER 24, 1931

Norman Rockwell
NOVEMBER 7, 1931

John E. Sheridan
NOVEMBER 14, 1931

E. M. Jackson
NOVEMBER 21, 1931

John LaGatta
DECEMBER 5, 1931

Norman Rockwell
DECEMBER 12, 1931

J. F. Kernan
DECEMBER 19, 1931

J. C. Leyendecker
DECEMBER 26, 1931

J. C. Leyendecker
JANUARY 2, 1932

Ellen Pyle
JANUARY 9, 1932

Tempest Inman
JANUARY 16, 1932

Anton Otto Fischer
JANUARY 23, 1932

Norman Rockwell
JANUARY 30, 1932

John E. Sheridan
FEBRUARY 6, 1932

Charles Edward Chambers
FEBRUARY 13, 1932

Henry J. Soulen
FEBRUARY 20, 1932

John LaGatta
FEBRUARY 27, 1932

J. C. Leyendecker
MARCH 5, 1932

Ellen Pyle
MARCH 12, 1932

Lynn Bogue Hunt
MARCH 19, 1932

J. C. Leyendecker
MARCH 26, 1932

John LaGatta
APRIL 2, 1932

Anton Otto Fischer
APRIL 9, 1932

McClelland Barclay
APRIL 16, 1932

Frank Lea
APRIL 23, 1932

Penrhyn Stanlaws
APRIL 30, 1932

Ellen Pyle
MAY 7, 1932

J. C. Leyendecker
MAY 14, 1932

Henry J. Soulen
MAY 21, 1932

J. F. Kernan
MAY 28, 1932

J. C. Leyendecker
JUNE 4, 1932

Eugene Iverd
JUNE 11, 1932

Tempest Inman
JUNE 18, 1932

Jack Murray
JUNE 25, 1932

J. C. Leyendecker
JULY 2, 1932

Penrhyn Stanlaws
JULY 9, 1932

Gordon Grant
JULY 16, 1932

Charles Hargens
JULY 23, 1932

Guy Hoff
JULY 30, 1932

J. C. Leyendecker
AUGUST 6, 1932

Lynn Bogue Hunt
AUGUST 13, 1932

Ellen Pyle
AUGUST 20, 1932

Eugene Iverd
AUGUST 27, 1932

J. C. Leyendecker
SEPTEMBER 3, 1932

Edgar Franklin Wittmack
SEPTEMBER 10, 1932

Guy Hoff
SEPTEMBER 17, 1932

J. C. Leyendecker
SEPTEMBER 24, 1932

J. F. Kernan
OCTOBER 1, 1932

John E. Sheridan
OCTOBER 8, 1932

J. F. Kernan
OCTOBER 15, 1932

Norman Rockwell
OCTOBER 22, 1932

W. Wilkinson
OCTOBER 29, 1932

Tempest Inman
NOVEMBER 5, 1932

Ellen Pyle
NOVEMBER 12, 1932

John E. Sheridan
NOVEMBER 19, 1932

Norman Rockwell
DECEMBER 10, 1932

Ellen Pyle
DECEMBER 17, 1932

J. C. Leyendecker
DECEMBER 24, 1932

J. C. Leyendecker
DECEMBER 31, 1932

Eugene Iverd
JANUARY 7, 1933

Jack Murray
JANUARY 14, 1933

Guy Hoff
JANUARY 21, 1933

Douglass Crockwell
JANUARY 28, 1933

Charles W. Dennis
FEBRUARY 4, 1933

Edgar Franklin Wittmack
FEBRUARY 11, 1933

C. Gager Phillips
FEBRUARY 18, 1933

J. C. Leyendecker
FEBRUARY 25, 1933

Charles Hargens
MARCH 4, 1933

Marland Stone
MARCH 11, 1933

Anton Otto Fischer
MARCH 18, 1933

Edgar Franklin Wittmack
MARCH 25, 1933

Alfred F. Cammarata
APRIL 1, 1933

Norman Rockwell
APRIL 8, 1933

J. C. Leyendecker
APRIL 15, 1933

Penrhyn Stanlaws
APRIL 22, 1933

Jack Murray
APRIL 29, 1933

Harold Anderson
MAY 6, 1933

Charles W. Dennis
MAY 13, 1933

Anton Otto Fischer
MAY 20, 1933

W. H. D. Koerner
MAY 27, 1933

George W. Gage
JUNE 3, 1933

Leopold Seyffert
JUNE 10, 1933

Norman Rockwell
JUNE 17, 1933

Eugene Iverd
JUNE 24, 1933

J. C. Leyendecker
JULY 1, 1933

John LaGatta
JULY 8, 1933

Howard Van Dyck
JULY 15, 1933

Penrhyn Stanlaws
JULY 22, 1933

Russell Sambrook
JULY 29, 1933

Norman Rockwell
AUGUST 5, 1933

Wladyslaw Theodor Benda
AUGUST 12, 1933

Penrhyn Stanlaws
AUGUST 19, 1933

J. C. Leyendecker
AUGUST 26, 1933

151

Paul Bransom
SEPTEMBER 2, 1933

John LaGatta
SEPTEMBER 9, 1933

J. C. Leyendecker
SEPTEMBER 16, 1933

Penrhyn Stanlaws
SEPTEMBER 23, 1933

Alan Foster
SEPTEMBER 30, 1933

Edgar Franklin Wittmack
OCTOBER 7, 1933

Robert C. Kauffmann
OCTOBER 14, 1933

Norman Rockwell
OCTOBER 21, 1933

Jack Murray
OCTOBER 28, 1933

J. C. Leyendecker
NOVEMBER 4, 1933

Harold Anderson
NOVEMBER 11, 1933

Wladyslaw Theodor Benda
NOVEMBER 18, 1933

Norman Rockwell
NOVEMBER 25, 1933

J. C. Leyendecker
DECEMBER 2, 1933

Tempest Inman
DECEMBER 9, 1933

Norman Rockwell
DECEMBER 16, 1933

J. C. Leyendecker
DECEMBER 23, 1933

John LaGatta
JANUARY 6, 1934

J. F. Kernan
JANUARY 13, 1934

Tom Webb
JANUARY 20, 1934

Walter Beach Humphrey
JANUARY 27, 1934

Penrhyn Stanlaws
FEBRUARY 3, 1934

Frederic Mizen
FEBRUARY 10, 1934

Bradshaw Crandall
FEBRUARY 17, 1934

Edgar Franklin Wittmach
FEBRUARY 24, 1934

W. H. D. Koerner
MARCH 3, 1934

J. C. Leyendecker
MARCH 10, 1934

Norman Rockwell
MARCH 17, 1934

Eugene Iverd
MARCH 24, 1934

J. C. Leyendecker
MARCH 31, 1934

Frederic Mizen
APRIL 7, 1934

Penrhyn Stanlaws
APRIL 14, 1934

153

Norman Rockwell
APRIL 21, 1934

John Newton Howitt
APRIL 28, 1934

Ellen Pyle
MAY 5, 1934

Wladyslaw Theodor Benda
MAY 12, 1934

Norman Rockwell
MAY 19, 1934

J. C. Leyendecker
MAY 26, 1934

Bradshaw Crandall
JUNE 2, 1934

Maurice Bower
JUNE 9, 1934

Penrhyn Stanlaws
JUNE 16, 1934

J. F. Kernan
JUNE 23, 1934

Norman Rockwell
JUNE 30, 1934

J. C. Leyendecker
JULY 7, 1934

John LaGatta
JULY 14, 1934

Eugene Iverd
JULY 21, 1934

Edgar Franklin Wittmack
JULY 28, 1934

Maurice Bower
AUGUST 4, 1934

Charles A. MacLellan
AUGUST 11, 1934

Eugene Iverd
AUGUST 18, 1934

Jack Murray
AUGUST 25, 1934

F. Sands Brunner
SEPTEMBER 1, 1934

Anton Otto Fischer
SEPTEMBER 8, 1934

J. C. Leyendecker
SEPTEMBER 15, 1934

Norman Rockwell
SEPTEMBER 22, 1934

Gordon Grant
SEPTEMBER 29, 1934

Eugene Iverd
OCTOBER 6, 1934

Charles W. Dennis
OCTOBER 13, 1934

Norman Rockwell
OCTOBER 20, 1934

Edgar Franklin Wittmack
OCTOBER 27, 1934

Eugene Iverd
NOVEMBER 3, 1934

J. F. Kernan
NOVEMBER 10, 1934

Eugene Iverd
NOVEMBER 17, 1934

Ellen Pyle
NOVEMBER 24, 1934

J. C. Leyendecker
DECEMBER 1, 1934

John E. Sheridan
DECEMBER 8, 1934

Norman Rockwell
DECEMBER 15, 1934

Mary Ellen Sigsbee
DECEMBER 22, 1934

Maurice Bower
JANUARY 12, 1935

John LaGatta
JANUARY 19, 1935

Douglass Crockwell
JANUARY 26, 1935

Edgar Franklin Wittmack
FEBRUARY 2, 1935

Norman Rockwell
FEBRUARY 9, 1935

F. Sands Brunner
FEBRUARY 16, 1935

J. C. Leyendecker
FEBRUARY 23, 1935

Bradshaw Crandall
MARCH 2, 1935

Norman Rockwell
MARCH 9, 1935

Ellen Pyle
MARCH 16, 1935

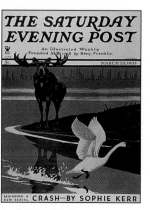

Jacob Bates Abbott
MARCH 23, 1935

Anton Otto Fischer
MARCH 30, 1935

Maurice Bower
APRIL 6, 1935

Bradshaw Crandall
APRIL 13, 1935

J. C. Leyendecker
APRIL 20, 1935

Norman Rockwell
APRIL 27, 1935

Maurice Bower
MAY 4, 1935

J. C. Leyendecker
MAY 11, 1935

Cushman Parker
MAY 18, 1935

Earle K. Bergey
MAY 25, 1935

Maurice Bower
JUNE 1, 1935

J. C. Leyendecker
JUNE 8, 1935

William Andrew Loomis
JUNE 15, 1935

Eugene Iverd
JUNE 22, 1935

Edgar Franklin Wittmack
JUNE 29, 1935

J. C. Leyendecker
JULY 6, 1935

Norman Rockwell
JULY 13, 1935

Walt Otto
JULY 20, 1935

157

J. F. Kernan
JULY 27, 1935

Guy Hoff
AUGUST 3, 1935

George Brehm
AUGUST 10, 1935

Maurice Bower
AUGUST 17, 1935

Guy Hoff
AUGUST 24, 1935

J. F. Kernan
AUGUST 31, 1935

Penrhyn Stanlaws
SEPTEMBER 7, 1935

Norman Rockwell
SEPTEMBER 14, 1935

Ellen Pyle
SEPTEMBER 21, 1935

J. C. Leyendecker
SEPTEMBER 28, 1935

Gordon Grant
OCTOBER 5, 1935

Maurice Bower
OCTOBER 12, 1935

J. C. Leyendecker
OCTOBER 19, 1935

Penrhyn Stanlaws
OCTOBER 26, 1935

Frederic Stanley
NOVEMBER 2, 1935

J. F. Kernan
NOVEMBER 9, 1935

158

Norman Rockwell
NOVEMBER 16, 1935

J. C. Leyendecker
NOVEMBER 23, 1935

Albert W. Hampson
NOVEMBER 30, 1935

R. J. Cavaliere
DECEMBER 7, 1935

Edgar Franklin Wittmack
DECEMBER 14, 1935

Norman Rockwell
DECEMBER 21, 1935

J. C. Leyendecker
JANUARY 4, 1936

Monte Crews
JANUARY 11, 1936

Maurice Bower
JANUARY 18, 1936

Norman Rockwell
JANUARY 25, 1936

Jack Murray
FEBRUARY 1, 1936

Henrietta McCaig Starrett
FEBRUARY 8, 1936

J. C. Leyendecker
FEBRUARY 15, 1936

Ellen Pyle
FEBRUARY 22, 1936

Maurice Bower
FEBRUARY 29, 1936

Norman Rockwell
MARCH 7, 1936

R. J. Cavaliere
MARCH 14, 1936

Anton Otto Fischer
MARCH 21, 1936

Ellen Pyle
MARCH 28, 1936

W. H. D. Koerner
APRIL 4, 1936

J. C. Leyendecker
APRIL 11, 1936

James C. McKell
APRIL 18, 1936

Norman Rockwell
APRIL 25, 1936

Henry J. Soulen
MAY 2, 1936

Charles R. Chickering
MAY 9, 1936

R. J. Cavaliere
MAY 16, 1936

Albert W. Hampson
MAY 23, 1936

Norman Rockwell
MAY 30, 1936

Frances Tipton Hunter
JUNE 6, 1936

Maurice Bower
JUNE 13, 1936

J. C. Leyendecker
JUNE 20, 1936

Robert C. Kauffmann
JUNE 27, 1936

J. C. Leyendecker
JULY 4, 1936

Norman Rockwell
JULY 11, 1936

Charles A. MacLellan
JULY 18, 1936

R. J. Cavaliere
JULY 25, 1936

Eugene Iverd
AUGUST 1, 1936

J. F. Kernan
AUGUST 8, 1936

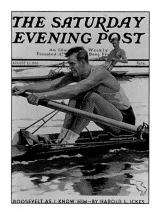

Maurice Bower
AUGUST 15, 1936

Charles Hergens
AUGUST 22, 1936

Albert W. Hampson
AUGUST 29, 1936

Maurice Bower
SEPTEMBER 5, 1936

Frances Tipton Hunter
SEPTEMBER 12, 1936

Mortimer Hyman
SEPTEMBER 19, 1936

Norman Rockwell
SEPTEMBER 26, 1936

Leslie Thrasher
OCTOBER 3, 1936

Rowland E. Wintchuff
OCTOBER 10, 1936

Norman Rockwell
OCTOBER 24, 1936

George W. Gage
OCTOBER 31, 1936

Edgar Franklin Wittmack
NOVEMBER 7, 1936

Monte Crews
NOVEMBER 14, 1936

J. C. Leyendecker
NOVEMBER 28, 1936

Frances Tipton Hunter
DECEMBER 5, 1936

John Newton Howitt
DECEMBER 12, 1936

Norman Rockwell
DECEMBER 19, 1936

J. C. Leyendecker
DECEMBER 26, 1936

J. C. Leyendecker
JANUARY 2, 1937

Monte Crews
JANUARY 9, 1937

Leslie Thrasher
JANUARY 16, 1937

Norman Rockwell
JANUARY 23, 1937

Paul Bransom
JANUARY 30, 1937

Maurice Bower
FEBRUARY 6, 1937

Tom Webb
FEBRUARY 13, 1937

J. C. Leyendecker
FEBRUARY 20, 1937

Frances Tipton Hunter
FEBRUARY 27, 1937

V. Keppler
MARCH 6, 1937

Tom Webb
MARCH 13, 1937

Douglass Crockwell
MARCH 20, 1937

J. C. Leyendecker
MARCH 27, 1937

McCauley Conner
APRIL 3, 1937

John LaGatta
APRIL 10, 1937

Jack Murray
APRIL 17, 1937

Norman Rockwell
APRIL 24, 1937

W. D. Stevens
MAY 1, 1937

John E. Sheridan
MAY 8, 1937

J. C. Leyendecker
MAY 15, 1937

NONL. C.CWS
MAY 22, 1937

JUNE 5, 1937

JUNE 12, 1937

JUNE 19, 1937

Ruzzie Green
JUNE 26, 1937

J. C. Leyendecker
JULY 3, 1937

Frances Tipton Hunter
JULY 10, 1937

John LaGatta
JULY 17, 1937

Albert W. Hampson
JULY 24, 1937

Norman Rockwell
JULY 31, 1937

Ivan Dmitri
AUGUST 7, 1937

William J. Bailey
AUGUST 14, 1937

Alfred Panepinto
AUGUST 21, 1937

John LaGatta
AUGUST 28, 1937

Clayton Knight
SEPTEMBER 4, 1937

Robert C. Kauffmann
SEPTEMBER 11, 1937

J. C. Leyendecker
SEPTEMBER 18, 1937

August Schombrug
SEPTEMBER 25, 1937

Norman Rockwell
OCTOBER 2, 1937

Frances Tipton Hunter
OCTOBER 9, 1937

John E. Sheridan
OCTOBER 16, 1937

E. M. Jackson
OCTOBER 23, 1937

Robert B. Velie
OCTOBER 30, 1937

J. C. Leyendecker
NOVEMBER 6, 1937

John E. Sheridan
NOVEMBER 13, 1937

Ski Weld
NOVEMBER 20, 1937

Frances Tipton Hunter
NOVEMBER 27, 1937

Michael Dolas
DECEMBER 4, 1937

Douglass Crockwell
DECEMBER 11, 1937

J. C. Leyendecker
DECEMBER 18, 1937

Norman Rockwell
DECEMBER 25, 1937

J. C. Leyendecker
JANUARY 1, 1938

Jack Murray
JANUARY 8, 1938

V. Kupplor
JANUARY 15, 1938

Albert W. Hampson
JANUARY 22, 1938

Francis Lee Jaques
JANUARY 29, 1938

Edgar Franklin Wittmack
FEBRUARY 5, 1938

J. C. Leyendecker
FEBRUARY 12, 1938

Norman Rockwell
FEBRUARY 19, 1938

Ski Weld
FEBRUARY 26, 1938

Frances Tipton Hunter
MARCH 5, 1938

Samul Nelson Abbott
MARCH 12, 1938

John Newton Howitt
MARCH 19, 1938

Neysa McMein
MARCH 26, 1938

Russell Sambrook
APRIL 2, 1938

Ski Weld
APRIL 9, 1938

J. C. Leyendecker
APRIL 16, 1938

Norman Rockwell
APRIL 23, 1938

Frances Tipton Hunter
APRIL 30, 1938

John E. Sheridan
MAY 7, 1938

Ivan Dmitri
MAY 14, 1938

Neysa McMein
MAY 21, 1938

VALEDICTORY

Samul Nelson Abbott
MAY 28, 1938

Norman Rockwell
JUNE 4, 1938

THE ROMAN KID—By PAUL GALLICO

John Newton Howitt
JUNE 11, 1938

RAINBOW IN THE DESERT—By J. B. PRIESTLEY

Frances Arnold
JUNE 18, 1938

PRICE DAY • DOROTHY THOMAS • LELAND JAMIESON

Michael Dolas
JUNE 25, 1938

BEGINNING MR. MOTO IS SO SORRY—By J. P. MARQUAND

William Heaslip
JULY 2, 1938

J. P. McEVOY • PAUL GALLICO
COMMUNISM PRESSES ITS PANTS—By STANLEY HIGH

Douglass Crockwell
JULY 9, 1938

MORE WILL LIVE
THE STORY OF CHARLES A. LINDBERGH AND ALEXIS CARREL

Russell Sambrook
JULY 23, 1938

John LaGatta
JULY 30, 1938

CLARENCE BUDINGTON KELLAND • ALVA JOHNSTON

Paul Hesse
AUGUST 6, 1938

WINCHELL—By J. P. McEVOY

Douglass Crockwell
AUGUST 13, 1938

BEGINNING THREE BRIGHT PEBBLES—By LESLIE FORD

J. C. Leyendecker
AUGUST 20, 1938

THE THIRD PARTY GETS A RICH UNCLE

Tullus Moessel
SEPTEMBER 3, 1938

BEGINNING SECOND MEETING—By LUCIAN CARY

Robert C. Kauffmann
SEPTEMBER 10, 1938

BEGINNING MY DAY IN COURT—By ARTHUR TRAIN

Ski Weld
SEPTEMBER 17, 1938

PIGSKIN PREVIEW OF 1938

Frances Tipton Hunter
SEPTEMBER 24, 1938

Wesley Neff
OCTOBER 1, 1938

J. C. Leyendecker
OCTOBER 15, 1938

Lonie Bee
OCTOBER 22, 1938

Jack Murray
OCTOBER 29, 1938

Douglass Crockwell
NOVEMBER 5, 1938

John E. Sheridan
NOVEMBER 12, 1938

Norman Rockwell
NOVEMBER 19, 1938

J. C. Leyendecker
NOVEMBER 26, 1938

Neysa McMein
DECEMBER 3, 1938

Frances Tipton Hunter
DECEMBER 10, 1938

Norman Rockwell
DECEMBER 17, 1938

J. C. Leyendecker
DECEMBER 24, 1938

J. C. Leyendecker
DECEMBER 31, 1938

Neysa McMein
JANUARY 7, 1939

Douglass Crockwell
JANUARY 14, 1939

Paul Bransom
JANUARY 21, 1939

Walt Otto
JANUARY 28, 1939

Josef Kotula
FEBRUARY 4, 1939

Norman Rockwell
FEBRUARY 11, 1939

Ski Weld
FEBRUARY 18, 1939

J. C. Leyendecker
FEBRUARY 25, 1939

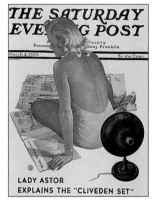

Robert P. Archer
MARCH 4, 1939

Julius Moessel
MARCH 11, 1939

Norman Rockwell
MARCH 18, 1939

Frances Tipton Hunter
MARCH 25, 1939

J. C. Leyendecker
APRIL 1, 1939

Douglass Crockwell
APRIL 8, 1939

Emery Clarke
APRIL 15, 1939

John R. Sheridan
APRIL 22, 1939

Norman Rockwell
APRIL 29, 1939

John Hyde Phillips
MAY 6, 1939

Douglas H. Hilliker
MAY 13, 1939

John LaGatta
MAY 20, 1939

Douglass Crockwell
MAY 27, 1939

John E. Sheridan
JUNE 3, 1939

Jacob Bates Abbott
JUNE 10, 1939

Philip Clay Roettinger
JUNE 17, 1939

John LaGatta
JUNE 24, 1939

Arthur H. Fisher
JULY 1, 1939

Norman Rockwell
JULY 8, 1939

Emery Clarke
JULY 15, 1939

Paul Hesse
JULY 22, 1939

Floyd Davis
JULY 29, 1939

Norman Rockwell
AUGUST 5, 1939

John Hyde Phillips
AUGUST 12, 1939

Frances Tipton Hunter
AUGUST 19, 1939

Charles E. Kerlee
AUGUST 26, 1939

Norman Rockwell
SEPTEMBER 2, 1939

BEGINNING A MACKINLAY KANTOR SERIAL

McCauley Conner
SEPTEMBER 9, 1939

MERCHANDISING MIRACLES By ALSOP AND KINTNER

Frances Tipton Hunter
SEPTEMBER 16, 1939

PIGSKIN PREVIEW OF 1939

Crosby DeMoss
SEPTEMBER 23, 1939

DON'T ASK QUESTIONS By J. P. MARQUAND

Monte Crews
SEPTEMBER 30, 1939

COLUMBIA, THE GEM OF THE OCEAN by FLETCHER PRATT

Ivan Dmitri
OCTOBER 7, 1939

STALIN OVER EUROPE By DEMAREE BESS

H. Wilson Smith
OCTOBER 14, 1939

WINSTON CHURCHILL By VINCENT SHEEAN

A. F. Sozio
OCTOBER 21, 1939

BATTLE STATIONS! By ALEC HUDSON
WE MUST KEEP OUT By HERBERT HOOVER

Douglass Crockwell
OCTOBER 28, 1939

THE STORY OF HELEN HAYES

Norman Rockwell
NOVEMBER 4, 1939

BEGINNING A FOOTBALL SERIAL

Lonie Bee
NOVEMBER 18, 1939

MARJORIE KINNAN RAWLINGS · MACKINLAY KANTOR

J. C. Leyendecker
NOVEMBER 25, 1939

CAN THEY BOMB US? By FLETCHER PRATT

H. Wilson Smith
DECEMBER 2, 1939

BEGINNING HIGH FRONTIER By LELAND JAMIESON

Jack Murray
DECEMBER 9, 1939

BEGINNING A SERIAL BY CLARENCE BUDINGTON KELLAND

Norman Rockwell
DECEMBER 16, 1939

THOMASON · WYLIE · ALEXANDER

J. C. Leyendecker
DECEMBER 23, 1939

IS RUSSIA WINNING CHINA TOO?

J. C. Leyendecker
DECEMBER 30, 1939

Norman Rockwell
MARCH 6, 1948

CHAPTER 5

THE FORTIES

On the covers of the *Saturday Evening Post*, World War II looked very different from World War I. Gone were Leyendecker's handsome doughboys charming Belgian orphans and leading captured turkeys back to camp for Thanksgiving. Gone, too, were the Red Cross nurses and gold-star parents. As it had in 1917, the *Post* shouldered the patriotic burden of supporting a war it had long resisted, but by 1941 the *Post*, like America, was far less innocent and in most ways less sentimental.

One familiar icon of the earlier war remained, if only for a while. Up to the beginning of 1943 the Leyendecker baby continued to announce the New Year and to express himself on the subject of war. In

1941, as isolationist as the *Post*, the squalling baby has been hoisted from behind, his diaper grasped in a mailed fist (January 4). The New Year's issue for 1942 postdated Pearl Harbor by a month, but Leyendecker's cover had been prepared earlier. Still isolationist but now prepared, the baby carries a rifle and crouches on the globe, defending North America. A broad No Trespassing sign covers the western hemisphere (January 3). Leyendecker's last cover for the *Post* appeared on January 2, 1943. The New Year baby is now at war. Helmeted and athletic, he bayonets a Nazi swastika.

Leyendecker had represented the first war for the *Post*; now Norman Rockwell assumed the premier role in depicting World War II. Thus, when the New Year baby was retired, it was Rockwell who painted the New Year's cover for January 1, 1944. Appropriately, that cover continued the story of Rockwell's own G. I. Joe, Willie Gillis. In the history of Willie Gillis, Rockwell found the figure to express a resolute and good-natured response to war.

Willie Gillis made his first appearance on October 4, 1941. He is not Leyendecker's tall and strong-jawed hero, but a little guy, even a bit funny-looking. In this first cover, Private Gillis has received a package of food from home, and he finds himself followed closely by half a dozen larger, eager-looking soldiers, all of whom outrank him.

Willie's war is a cheerful war. There are no scenes of battle, and the closest he comes to danger is to find himself in a blackout, alone in the dark with a pretty young woman (June 27, 1942). In fact, despite his small frame and ordinary face, Willie is a success with women. On the February 7, 1942, cover, two USO workers hover over a seated Willie, plying him with coffee and doughnuts. On September 5 of that year, a similar composition was used, with two young women facing off over their mailboxes; each has received a photograph of Willie. There are solemn moments as well. In another 1942 cover, Willie is seated in church; he is somewhat isolated, for of the rest of the congregation we see only the arm of a sergeant. Willie is solemn and thoughtful (July 25; page 180, top left).

Not only did Rockwell create Willie Gillis, but Rosie the Riveter as well. Although she appeared on only one cover, both her image and her name became icons. Like Willie, Rosie has an ordinary face; there is no glamour here. In the famous cover of May 29, 1943, Rosie appears perched atop a pole, eating a sandwich (page 180, top right). Her position and form are borrowed from Michelangelo's Prophet Isaiah,* and she is accordingly strong and well-muscled. Her chest is covered with medals, and across her overall-clad legs lies her riveting gun.

Rockwell also sent a cousin of Rosie's to war on the home front, on the September 4, 1943, cover (page 180, bottom left). Hung about with an extraordinary array of gear, Liberty Girl is dressed in Uncle Sam's stars and stripes, and strides off to do her bit in dozens of wartime jobs, both those that are traditionally female and those that had long been male preserves. As her various implements indicate, Liberty Girl is ready for work as boardinghouse keeper, a chambermaid, a telephone operator, a milk truck driver, a seamstress, a baggage clerk, a bus or taxi driver, a nurse, a farmworker, and more.

Rockwell's war was not always so blithe. His *Four Freedoms*, reproduced within the magazine, have become American classics, but even on the *Post* cover he took on more solemn subjects. One cover

*Thomas S. Buechner, *Norman Rockwell, Artist and Illustrator* (New York: Harry N. Abrams, 1970), figures 354 and 356.

demonstrates vividly the distance from World War I: a disabled veteran stares at the war bond he has just purchased. Certainly the veteran looks strong and fit; only his crutch tells us he has been hurt (July 1, 1944). Nevertheless, even an implied wound represents a new concession to realism. Rockwell painted a particularly moving cover for Thanksgiving in 1943 (page 180, bottom right). Amid shambles, a young refugee woman kneels at prayer; against the cold she wears the jacket, huge on her small frame, of a United States Army sergeant (November 27).

The *Post* also represented the war through the work of Mead Schaeffer (page 181). His first cover appeared on September 12, 1942, a dramatic picture of a crouching paratrooper about to jump from a plane. Over the next two years, Schaeffer did more than a dozen covers celebrating different branches of the armed services. He always showed a man, occasionally accompanied by his fellows, close up and in action. An infantry man moves through the jungle. A sailor stands watch. A kneeling signal corpsman talks over a field radio. An anti-aircraft gunner positions his artillery. A medic tends to a fallen soldier (October 24 and November 7, 1942; September 9, February 5, and March 11, 1944). Schaeffer's war is a drama of heroic men dedicated to their particular duties.

Numerous other war covers were contributed. Ivan Dmitri's last work for the *Post* was photographs of a flight squadron and of a bomber (May 16 and August 29, 1942). The navy sent official photographs, one of a pilot shooting from a helicopter, another of a sailor signaling with flags (April 10, 1943; May 17, 1941). Alongside this realism were examples of sentiment and humor. A beautifully smiling nurse gives a cigarette to a handsome, contented, and—one as-

sumes—wounded soldier. Another handsome soldier feeds his pretty date a hot dog. A disappointed sailor holds up for our inspection the garish tie sent him by Aunt Millie (October 23, 1943; October 10 and May 23, 1942).

The war's end brought homecoming covers, especially from the hand of Rockwell. Back home, one soldier helps his mother prepare Thanksgiving dinner, and another finds that his civilian clothes no longer fit him. Still another sits silent, a souvenir Japanese flag in his hands, as a group of men and boys urges him to tell of his adventures (November 24, December 15, and October 13, 1945). Rockwell's most affecting homecoming cover was painted for the issue of May 26, 1945. It is dominated by the facade of a tenement house; from the doors, out of the windows, over the fence, and even down the straggly tree come shouts of welcome. Behind the corner of the building a shy girlfriend waits; with his back to us, standing still and straight, the ordinary private—a redheaded first cousin to Willie Gillis—comes home. And Willie came home, too, on October 5, 1946. We see him last, a better-looking and manlier Willie, on a window seat, smoking a pipe and reading. Willie Gillis has entered college.

Mead Schaeffer, too, produced a homecoming cover, a curious echo of Charles MacLellan's painting of a rural homecoming in 1919. Against the background of an enormous mountain wall, a road curves around to a farm homestead in the distance. In the foreground, in an old-fashioned horse-drawn buckboard, the farm family brings home their sailor son (August 25, 1945)

In 1942, in the middle of the war, the *Post* changed editors, and Ben Hibbs replaced Wesley Stout. One result was a dramatic change in the covers of the magazine.

The logo was altered so that the single word "POST" dominated the upper left, with "The Saturday Evening" in small type above; and the typeface was modernized. As *Time* magazine put it, "The cover was redesigned to eliminate all memories of the past but Norman Rockwell."* Less immediately obvious but perhaps more important over time, Hibbs altered Stout's basic policy about cover artists.

During his time as editor, Stout had experimented continually with the work of new cover artists. Often an artist painted no more than one or two covers. As a result, between 1940 and 1945 the work of over seventy-five different artists appeared on the *Post* cover. With the end of the war and Hibbs firmly in control, all this altered. From 1946 through 1949, only sixteen artists drew *Post* covers, and of these, eight were responsible for all but fifteen cover illustrations. The result of this change was a much more standardized and recognizable cover style. To be sure, each of these eight artists had his own distinctive style. There was variety but, given the frequency with which each artist's work appeared, the result was a sense of familiarity.

Rockwell, of course, remained the preeminent, though no longer the most frequent, cover artist for the magazine. Several of his covers from these years are among his best and best-known work. Two cleaning women rest in theater seats studying the evening's program. A defeated baseball team slumps in the dugout; above its roof we see the ecstatic fans cheering the other team. The Rockwell family gathers for Christmas. Three grim umpires must decide whether to call the game for rain (April 6, 1946; September 4 and December 25, 1948; April 23, 1949—page 179). And in the brilliant "Gossip," painted for the March 6, 1948, cover (page 172), a series of paired heads traces the course of a rumor, from the woman who starts it to the same woman, who hears it at the end from the very angry man about whom she gossiped in the beginning. In these years Rockwell was featured inside the *Post* as well as on its covers. Between 1946 and 1948 he did his well-known series of *Visits*: to a Country Editor, a Family Doctor, and a County Agent.

The other leading cover artists for the *Post*, despite the variety in their styles and in the approaches they took to their subject matter, shared a commitment to rendering aspects of American life and the American landscape. Following the war, the *Post* turned to a celebration of America. Along with recapitulations of the war in the form of memoir or Monday-morning quarterbacking, and along with a growing obsession with Russia and Communism, the magazine began featuring frequent articles on American cities. This series ran for years, moving slowly from the great cities of the nation to the small and insignificant. The same desire to focus on things American marked the cover art.

Stevan Dohanos, the most frequent cover artist of the period, used a realistic approach toward a variety of representations of the American scene. Sometimes he painted ordinary places with extraordinary detail, offering postwar America the reassurance of the familiar. In a barber shop the barber gets a haircut, surrounded by the appropriate appointments, from barber pole to towels (January 26, 1946). The owner of a hardware store sets up his street display; the street and the display are filled with commonplace objects, from the U.S. Route 1 sign to the rack of garden implements (March 16, 1946). On other occasions he turned to small-town America, with a

Time, May 19, 1961.

lighted church door revealing a country choir practicing at night or a town square where the Christmas tree is being trimmed (August 10, 1946; December 4, 1948). He could exploit sentiment, as on the July 5, 1947, cover. A father and son, both veterans, are ready for the parade; the son in his World War II uniform waits at the foot of the front stoop, while on the porch stands his father in his World War I uniform with a furled flag under his arm, as his wife adjusts his tie. Dohanos could also provide wry humor. A baseball team waits on the sidewalk while the pitcher finishes mowing the lawn. Or a morose wife sits at the dining-room table surveying the cleanup to be done; her husband sits comfortably in his easy chair, reading the paper (July 20, 1946; January 8, 1949).

Mead Schaeffer turned from his figures of Americans at war to studies of rural America. For the November 25, 1944, cover he painted a barn dance, and the next year he rendered maple-syrup making in Vermont (February 17, 1945). But by 1946 he was again focusing on strong and realistic paintings of distinctly American men, now at work: a lobster man on a rough sea, men struggling to position an oil drill, moss pickers in a Louisiana bayou, shrimpers in Biloxi (March 9 and November 9, 1946; April 5 and October 25, 1947).

John Philip Falter was another popular realistic painter of *Post* covers who specialized in American scenes. Falter was adept at both rural and urban settings. Rural paintings were often set in his native Nebraska. He did a cover of Main Street in Falls City, Nebraska, at Christmas, a street scene shown from above (December 21, 1946). He also painted Lovers' Lane in Falls City, a dark painting of a rural landscape with small cars in the foreground (May 24, 1947). Other rural subjects included milk-

ing time at sunset, apple picking, and an evening picnic along the Missouri River (January 12, 1946; September 27, 1947; June 4, 1949). A particularly effective cover, for February 1, 1947, shows an expanse of snow-covered prairie; in the right foreground two small figures watch a school bus approach over the snowy road.

Falter's urban scenes were equally skilled. For New York, as for Falls City, he did a bird's-eye view (August 17, 1946). There were other versions of New York as well: Central Park after a rain, with the cityscape in the background; and a view of Saint Patrick's Cathedral and Rockefeller Center (April 30 and December 3, 1949). For the New Year's cover in 1948, Falter painted the facades of apartment houses; through the lighted windows we see glimpses of various New Year's Eve activities (January 3). An unusual cover, for April 19, 1947, takes up the subject of baseball, always a *Post* favorite. Falter provides a different view, more like that of a sports photographer: we see the game from the field level, behind third base, as the batter takes a roundhouse swing; in the background are the tiers of the stadium, filled with fans.

John Atherton, too, was a realistic painter. In 1944 and 1945, when he began doing *Post* covers, he did a number of still-life paintings. A fisherman's showed fish, fishing gear, and the fisherman's hat lying on the grass. A hunter's still life displayed a pheasant, a pouch, and other gear hung on the wall. His railway station still life has a pot-bellied stove in the center, surrounded by posted bills in various stages of decomposition. A study of rainwear on a coat rack takes on the same still-life quality (April 15, November 11, and December 2, 1944; April 14, 1945).

By 1946 Atherton had turned from still

lifes to renderings of American places. Typically, the subject of the painting was dwarfed by elements of nature. A paddle wheeler on the Ohio River, on the September 21, 1946, cover, sails in front of a looming hill. In some of his work, Atherton concentrated on the machinery of America. A picture of an ore mine in the Mesabi Range focuses on a derrick; seen from below, it is huge (November 22, 1947). Another, of a sawmill lumberyard in Oregon, provides nearly a Constructivist view, close up and from the front, of the stacked planks (April 10, 1948). A particularly dramatic celebration of the machine is his November 23, 1946, cover of Pittsburgh by night, with the glare from the furnaces outlining the steel plants on the river. Atherton, it should be noted, painted the annual Ben Franklin cover as well. By the early 1940s this mid-January cover had been regularized: a bronze bust of Franklin appears along with a scroll on which is lettered, in eighteenth-century style, some saying of Franklin's thought appropriate for the moment.

Not all the principal *Post* cover artists in the postwar years were realists. In Constantin Alajalov the magazine found a very different kind of stylist. Alajalov is most readily associated with *The New Yorker*, where he was long a favored cover artist. His stylized figures flirt with the possibilities of the cartoon, but remain sophisticated. If Alajalov's style is unusual for the *Post*, his subjects are not. He favored the humor that arises in moments of intense frustration. The April 13, 1946, cover shows a dinner party at a critical juncture. The host has decided to cook, and he is shown in the foreground breaking eggs into a bowl and reading a cookbook; behind him his wife and their guests wait, not particularly patiently. For Thanksgiving the following year he turned the tables. In the background, three people sit at the dining-room table, enjoying one another's company. In the foreground we find the hostess, staring with horror as she takes her burned and smoking turkey out of the oven (November 29, 1947). Another particularly successful cover shows a man in pajamas peering carefully around his partially opened front door; outside are his milk and his Sunday paper and, unfortunately, the local minister talking with some more devout parishioners (February 21, 1948).

No survey of the covers of the *Post* in the 1940s would be complete without a mention of Butch, the cocker spaniel whose mishaps and mischief were a staple. Butch was the creation of Albert Staehle, who later painted Smokey the Bear for the United States Forest Service. Butch first appeared on February 19, 1944, having eaten the ration coupons. A few months later, he was shown in a more patriotic vein, sleeping on an army jacket (June 10). But Butch's métier is trouble, and the covers usually featured him breaking a lamp, setting his muddy paws on a freshly laundered shirt, chewing up the mail (February 23, 1946; December 6, 1947; March 13, 1948). On the January 29, 1949, cover, he seems worth all the trouble, for he is sitting morosely in the lost-and-found department of a railroad station, ticketed like the luggage all around him.

By the end of the 1940s the covers of the *Post*, now principally the work of new and younger artists, had undergone great change. The holiday season for 1949 no longer featured the work of Leyendecker or of Rockwell. Instead it was Alajalov who rang in the new year on December 10, with a lonely waiter staring disconsolately at the party in progress in front of him.

Norman Rockwell
APRIL 23, 1949

Norman Rockwell
JULY 25, 1942

Norman Rockwell
MAY 29, 1943

Norman Rockwell
SEPTEMBER 4, 1943

Norman Rockwell
NOVEMBER 27, 1943

Mead Schaeffer
SEPTEMBER 12, 1942

Mead Schaeffer
FEBRUARY 5, 1944

Mead Schaeffer
SEPTEMBER 9, 1944

Mead Schaeffer
NOVEMBER 7, 1942

Paul Hesse
JANUARY 6, 1940

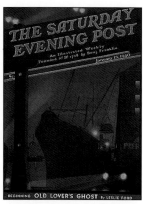

Ski Weld
JANUARY 13, 1940

J. C. Leyendecker
JANUARY 20, 1940

Dominice Cammerota
JANUARY 27, 1940

John Hyde Phillips
FEBRUARY 3, 1940

Ski Weld
FEBRUARY 10, 1940

Julius Moessel
FEBRUARY 17, 1940

Lincoln Borglum
FEBRUARY 24, 1940

Emery Clarke
MARCH 2, 1940

Arthur C. Radebaugh
MARCH 9, 1940

Albert W. Hampson
MARCH 16, 1940

J. C. Leyendecker
MARCH 23, 1940

Norman Rockwell
MARCH 30, 1940

Charles De Soria
APRIL 6, 1940

Emery Clarke
APRIL 13, 1940

Douglass Crockwell
APRIL 20, 1940

Norman Rockwell
APRIL 27, 1940

John Hyde Phillips
MAY 4, 1940

J. C. Leyendecker
MAY 11, 1940

Norman Rockwell
MAY 18, 1940

Frances Tipton Hunter
MAY 25, 1940

Paul Bransom
JUNE 1, 1940

Wynn Richards
JUNE 8, 1940

Miriam Troop
JUNE 15, 1940

Albert W. Hampson
JUNE 22, 1940

Ski Weld
JUNE 29, 1940

Douglass Crockwell
JULY 6, 1940

Norman Rockwell
JULY 13, 1940

Frances Tipton Hunter
JULY 20, 1940

Emery Clarke
JULY 27, 1940

Dominice Cammerota
AUGUST 3, 1940

Douglass Crockwell
AUGUST 10, 1940

Clyde H. Sunderland
AUGUST 17, 1940

Norman Rockwell
AUGUST 24, 1940

Albert W. Hampson
AUGUST 31, 1940

Werner Stoy
SEPTEMBER 7, 1940

John Hyde Phillips
SEPTEMBER 14, 1940

M. M. Herrick
SEPTEMBER 21, 1940

Walt Otto
SEPTEMBER 28, 1940

J. C. Leyendecker
OCTOBER 5, 1940

H. W. Smith
OCTOBER 12, 1940

John Newton Howitt
OCTOBER 19, 1940

Russell Sambrook
OCTOBER 26, 1940

William Edwin Booth
NOVEMBER 2, 1940

Miriam Troop
NOVEMBER 9, 1940

W. W. Calvert
NOVEMBER 16, 1940

Emery Clarke
NOVEMBER 23, 1940

Norman Rockwell
NOVEMBER 30, 1940

Emery Clarke
DECEMBER 7, 1940

John Hyde Phillips
DECEMBER 14, 1940

J. C. Leyendecker
DECEMBER 21, 1940

Norman Rockwell
DECEMBER 28, 1940

J. C. Leyendecker
JANUARY 4, 1941

Douglass Crockwell
JANUARY 11, 1941

Ski Weld
JANUARY 18, 1941

Emmett Watson
JANUARY 25, 1941

Albert W. Hampson
FEBRUARY 1, 1941

McClelland Barclay
FEBRUARY 8, 1941

Frances Tipton Hunter
FEBRUARY 15, 1941

Ski Weld
FEBRUARY 22, 1941

Norman Rockwell
MARCH 1, 1941

Jack Murray
MARCH 8, 1941

Lonie Bee
MARCH 15, 1941

John LaGatta
MARCH 22, 1941

Paul Bransom
MARCH 29, 1941

McCauley Conner
APRIL 5, 1941

Frances Tipton Hunter
APRIL 12, 1941

Emmett Watson
APRIL 19, 1941

John Hyde Phillips
APRIL 26, 1941

Norman Rockwell
MAY 3, 1941

Dominice Cammerota
MAY 10, 1941

United States Navy Photo
MAY 17, 1941

John Hyde Phillips
MAY 24, 1941

Sgt. Edward A. Lane
MAY 31, 1941

Rauschert J. Karl
JUNE 7, 1941

T. Patston
JUNE 14, 1941

Albert W. Hampson
JUNE 21, 1941

Roy Hilton
JUNE 28, 1941

Arthur C. Radebaugh
JULY 5, 1941

F. A. Leigh
JULY 12, 1941

Dale Nichols
JULY 19, 1941

Norman Rockwell
JULY 26, 1941

Ski Weld
AUGUST 2, 1941

John Hyde Phillips
AUGUST 9, 1941

Douglass Crockwell
AUGUST 16, 1941

Ski Weld
AUGUST 23, 1941

Charles Dye
AUGUST 30, 1941

John Hyde Phillips
SEPTEMBER 6, 1941

Ivan Dmitri
SEPTEMBER 13, 1941

Arthur C. Radebaugh
SEPTEMBER 20, 1941

Albert W. Hampson
SEPTEMBER 27, 1941

Norman Rockwell
OCTOBER 4, 1941

John LaGatta
OCTOBER 11, 1941

Lonie Bee
OCTOBER 18, 1941

Al Moore
OCTOBER 25, 1941

J. E. Reed
NOVEMBER 1, 1941

Howard Scott
NOVEMBER 8, 1941

Gene Pelham
NOVEMBER 15, 1941

R. E. Miller
NOVEMBER 22, 1941

Norman Rockwell
NOVEMBER 29, 1941

K. Severin
DECEMBER 6, 1941

Harold Werneke
DECEMBER 13, 1941

Norman Rockwell
DECEMBER 20, 1941

Miriam Tana Hoban
DECEMBER 27, 1941

J. C. Leyendecker
JANUARY 3, 1942

Ivan Dmitri
JANUARY 10, 1942

John Newton Howitt
JANUARY 17, 1942

Ski Weld
JANUARY 24, 1942

John Clymer
JANUARY 31, 1942

Norman Rockwell
FEBRUARY 7, 1942

Henry Waxman
FEBRUARY 14, 1942

Rudy Arnold
FEBRUARY 21, 1942

William Goadby Lawrence
FEBRUARY 28, 1942

Stevan Dohanos
MARCH 7, 1942

Dale Nichols
MARCH 14, 1942

Norman Rockwell
MARCH 21, 1942

Paul Bransom
MARCH 28, 1942

Douglass Crockwell
APRIL 4, 1942

Norman Rockwell
APRIL 11, 1942

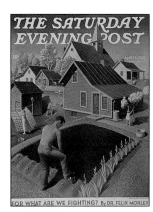

Grant Wood
APRIL 18, 1942

Gene Pelham
APRIL 25, 1942

Preston Duncan
MAY 2, 1942

W. W. Calvert
MAY 9, 1942

Ivan Dmitri
MAY 16, 1942

Charles Kaiser
MAY 23, 1942

Ruzzie Green
MAY 30, 1942

James W. Schucker
JUNE 6, 1942

W. W. Calvert
JUNE 13, 1942

Fred Ludekens
JUNE 20, 1942

Norman Rockwell
JUNE 27, 1942

John Clymer
JULY 4, 1942

Rudy Arnold
JULY 11, 1942

Paul Hesse
JULY 18, 1942

Rudy Arnold
AUGUST 1, 1942

Jon Whitcomb
AUGUST 8, 1942

Howard Scott
AUGUST 15, 1942

Charles Kaiser
AUGUST 22, 1942

Ivan Dmitri
AUGUST 29, 1942

Norman Rockwell
SEPTEMBER 5, 1942

Howard Scott
SEPTEMBER 19, 1942

Gilbert Bundy
SEPTEMBER 26, 1942

Arthur C. Radebaugh
OCTOBER 3, 1942

Al Moore
OCTOBER 10, 1942

W. W. Calvert
OCTOBER 17, 1942

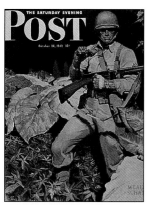

Mead Schaeffer
OCTOBER 24, 1942

Charles Kaiser
OCTOBER 31, 1942

Lonie Bee
NOVEMBER 14, 1942

Constance Bannister
NOVEMBER 21, 1942

Norman Rockwell
NOVEMBER 28, 1942

Howard Scott
DECEMBER 5, 1942

John Atherton
DECEMBER 12, 1942

Charles Kaiser
DECEMBER 19, 1942

Norman Rockwell
DECEMBER 26, 1942

J. C. Leyendecker
JANUARY 2, 1943

Mead Schaeffer
JANUARY 9, 1943

John Falter
JANUARY 16, 1943

Mat Kauten
JANUARY 23, 1943

W. W. Calvert
JANUARY 30, 1943

Ruzzie Green & John Sheridan
FEBRUARY 6, 1943

John Atherton
FEBRUARY 13, 1943

Mead Schaeffer
FEBRUARY 20, 1943

Howard Scott
FEBRUARY 27, 1943

Rutherford Boyd
MARCH 6, 1943

George Garland
MARCH 13, 1943

Charles Kaiser
MARCH 20, 1943

Mead Schaeffer
MARCH 27, 1943

Norman Rockwell
APRIL 3, 1943

United States Navy Official Photo
APRIL 10, 1943

Al Moore
APRIL 17, 1943

Ken Stuart
APRIL 24, 1943

Alex Ross
MAY 1, 1943

John Falter
MAY 8, 1943

Rutherford Boyd
MAY 15, 1943

Mead Schaeffer
MAY 22, 1943

Al Moore
JUNE 5, 1943

Mead Schaeffer
JUNE 12, 1943

Howard Scott
JUNE 19, 1943

Norman Rockwell
JUNE 26, 1943

John Atherton
JULY 3, 1943

John Falter
JULY 10, 1943

Rutherford Boyd
JULY 17, 1943

Alex Ross
JULY 24, 1943

Ken Stuart
JULY 31, 1943

Howard Scott
AUGUST 7, 1943

Ray Prohaska
AUGUST 14, 1943

Douglass Crockwell
AUGUST 21, 1943

Alex Ross
AUGUST 28, 1943

Rutherford Boyd
SEPTEMBER 11, 1943

Fred Ludekens
SEPTEMBER 18, 1943

John Atherton
SEPTEMBER 25, 1943

Russell Patterson
OCTOBER 2, 1943

Howard Scott
OCTOBER 9, 1943

Andrew Wyeth
OCTOBER 16, 1943

Jon Whitcomb
OCTOBER 23, 1943

John Hyde Phillips
OCTOBER 30, 1943

Mead Schaeffer
NOVEMBER 6, 1943

Ken Stuart
NOVEMBER 13, 1943

Robert Riggs
NOVEMBER 20, 1943

Stevan Dohanos
DECEMBER 4, 1943

Fred Ludekens
DECEMBER 11, 1943

John Atherton
DECEMBER 18, 1943

Mead Schaeffer
DECEMBER 25, 1943

Norman Rockwell
JANUARY 1, 1944

Stevan Dohanos
JANUARY 8, 1944

John Atherton
JANUARY 15, 1944

Howard Scott
JANUARY 22, 1944

Alex Ross
JANUARY 29, 1944

John Atherton
FEBRUARY 12, 1944

Albert Staehle
FEBRUARY 19, 1944

Fred Ludekens
FEBRUARY 26, 1944

Norman Rockwell
MARCH 4, 1944

Mead Schaeffer
MARCH 11, 1944

Rutherford Boyd
MARCH 18, 1944

John Falter
MARCH 25, 1944

Ken Stuart
APRIL 1, 1944

Alex Ross
APRIL 8, 1944

John Atherton
APRIL 15, 1944

Mead Schaeffer
APRIL 22, 1944

Norman Rockwell
APRIL 29, 1944

Howard Scott
MAY 6, 1944

Stevan Dohanos
MAY 13, 1944

Stan Ekman
MAY 20, 1944

Norman Rockwell
MAY 27, 1944

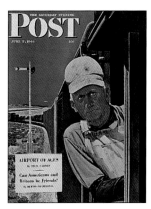

Fred Ludekens
JUNE 3, 1944

Albert Staehle
JUNE 10, 1944

Howard Scott
JUNE 17, 1944

Robert Riggs
JUNE 24, 1944

Norman Rockwell
JULY 1, 1944

John Atherton
JULY 8, 1944

Albert Staehle
JULY 15, 1944

Alex Ross
JULY 22, 1944

Stevan Dohanos
JULY 29, 1944

John Falter
AUGUST 5, 1944

Norman Rockwell
AUGUST 12, 1944

Fred Ludekens
AUGUST 19, 1944

John Atherton
AUGUST 26, 1944

Stevan Dohanos
SEPTEMBER 2, 1944

Norman Rockwell
SEPTEMBER 16, 1944

Stevan Dohanos
SEPTEMBER 23, 1944

John Falter
SEPTEMBER 30, 1944

Albert Staehle
OCTOBER 7, 1944

Howard Scott
OCTOBER 14, 1944

Stevan Dohanos
OCTOBER 21, 1944

Mead Schaeffer
OCTOBER 28, 1944

Norman Rockwell
NOVEMBER 4, 1944

John Atherton
NOVEMBER 11, 1944

Robert Riggs
NOVEMBER 18, 1944

Mead Schaeffer
NOVEMBER 25, 1944

John Atherton
DECEMBER 2, 1944

Stevan Dohanos
DECEMBER 9, 1944

John Falter
DECEMBER 16, 1944

Norman Rockwell
DECEMBER 23, 1944

Mead Schaeffer
DECEMBER 30, 1944

Stan Ekman
JANUARY 6, 1945

Stevan Dohanos
JANUARY 13, 1945

John Atherton
JANUARY 20, 1945

Howard Scott
JANUARY 27, 1945

John Atherton
FEBRUARY 3, 1945

Albert Staehle
FEBRUARY 10, 1945

Mead Schaeffer
FEBRUARY 17, 1945

John Atherton
FEBRUARY 24, 1945

Stevan Dohanos
MARCH 3, 1945

John Falter
MARCH 10, 1945

Norman Rockwell
MARCH 17, 1945

Stevan Dohanos
MARCH 24, 1945

Norman Rockwell
MARCH 31, 1945

John Falter
APRIL 7, 1945

John Atherton
APRIL 14, 1945

Stevan Dohanos
APRIL 21, 1945

Mead Schaeffer
APRIL 28, 1945

Alexander Brook
MAY 5, 1945

Stevan Dohanos
MAY 12, 1945

John Falter
MAY 19, 1945

Norman Rockwell
MAY 26, 1945

Allen Saalburg
JUNE 2, 1945

John Falter
JUNE 9, 1945

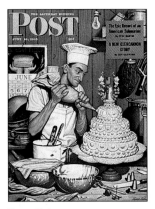

Stevan Dohanos
JUNE 16, 1945

Albert Staehle
JUNE 23, 1945

John Atherton
JUNE 30, 1945

John Falter
JULY 7, 1945

Stevan Dohanos
JULY 14, 1945

Fred Ludekens
JULY 21, 1945

Mead Schaeffer
JULY 28, 1945

Stevan Dohanos
AUGUST 4, 1945

Norman Rockwell
AUGUST 11, 1945

John Falter
AUGUST 18, 1945

Mead Schaeffer
AUGUST 25, 1945

Albert Staehle
SEPTEMBER 1, 1945

John Falter
SEPTEMBER 8, 1945

Norman Rockwell
SEPTEMBER 15, 1945

Stevan Dohanos
SEPTEMBER 22, 1945

Mead Schaeffer
SEPTEMBER 29, 1945

Constantin Alajalov
OCTOBER 6, 1945

Norman Rockwell
OCTOBER 13, 1945

John Falter
OCTOBER 20, 1945

John Atherton
OCTOBER 27, 1945

Norman Rockwell
NOVEMBER 3, 1945

Mead Schaeffer
NOVEMBER 10, 1945

Albert Staehle
NOVEMBER 17, 1945

Norman Rockwell
NOVEMBER 24, 1945

Stevan Dohanos
DECEMBER 1, 1945

John Falter
DECEMBER 8, 1945

Norman Rockwell
DECEMBER 15, 1945

James R. Bingham
DECEMBER 22, 1945

Norman Rockwell
DECEMBER 29, 1945

Stevan Dohanos
JANUARY 5, 1946

John Falter
JANUARY 12, 1946

John Atherton
JANUARY 19, 1946

Stevan Dohanos
JANUARY 26, 1946

Mead Schaeffer
FEBRUARY 2, 1946

Alexander Brook
FEBRUARY 9, 1946

Stevan Dohanos
FEBRUARY 16, 1946

Albert Staehle
FEBRUARY 23, 1946

Norman Rockwell
MARCH 2, 1946

Mead Schaeffer
MARCH 9, 1946

Stevan Dohanos
MARCH 16, 1946

John Falter
MARCH 23, 1946

John Atherton
MARCH 30, 1946

Norman Rockwell
APRIL 6, 1946

Constantin Alajalov
APRIL 13, 1946

E. Melbourne Brindle
APRIL 20, 1946

Stevan Dohanos
APRIL 27, 1946

Doris Lee
MAY 4, 1946

Albert Staehle
MAY 11, 1946

John Falter
MAY 18, 1946

John Atherton
MAY 25, 1946

Constantin Alajalov
JUNE 1, 1946

Albert Staehle
JUNE 8, 1946

Stevan Dohanos
JUNE 15, 1946

John Falter
JUNE 22, 1946

John Atherton
JUNE 29, 1946

Norman Rockwell
JULY 6, 1946

John Falter
JULY 13, 1946

Stevan Dohanos
JULY 20, 1946

Constantin Alajalov
JULY 27, 1946

Norman Rockwell
AUGUST 3, 1946

Stevan Dohanos
AUGUST 10, 1946

John Falter
AUGUST 17, 1946

Albert Staehle
AUGUST 24, 1946

Constantin Alajalov
AUGUST 31, 1946

Stevan Dohanos
SEPTEMBER 7, 1946

Mead Schaeffer
SEPTEMBER 14, 1946

John Atherton
SEPTEMBER 21, 1946

Albert Staehle
SEPTEMBER 28, 1946

Norman Rockwell
OCTOBER 5, 1946

John Falter
OCTOBER 12, 1946

Stevan Dohanos
OCTOBER 19, 1946

John Atherton
OCTOBER 26, 1946

Constantin Alajalov
NOVEMBER 2, 1946

Mead Schaeffer
NOVEMBER 9, 1946

Norman Rockwell
NOVEMBER 16, 1946

John Atherton
NOVEMBER 23, 1946

John Falter
NOVEMBER 30, 1946

Norman Rockwell
DECEMBER 7, 1946

Stevan Dohanos
DECEMBER 14, 1946

John Falter
DECEMBER 21, 1946

Mead Schaeffer
DECEMBER 28, 1946

Stevan Dohanos
JANUARY 4, 1947

Norman Rockwell
JANUARY 11, 1947

John Atherton
JANUARY 18, 1947

Constantin Alajalov
JANUARY 25, 1947

John Falter
FEBRUARY 1, 1947

Stevan Dohanos
FEBRUARY 8, 1947

Albert Staehle
FEBRUARY 15, 1947

John Atherton
FEBRUARY 22, 1947

John Falter
MARCH 1, 1947

Stevan Dohanos
MARCH 8, 1947

Constantin Alajalov
MARCH 15, 1947

2465 Norman Rockwell
MARCH 22, 1947

2466 John Falter
MARCH 29, 1947

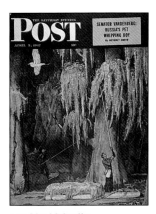

2467 Mead Schaeffer
APRIL 5, 1947

Stevan Dohanos
APRIL 12, 1947

John Falter
APRIL 19, 1947

John Atherton
APRIL 26, 1947

Norman Rockwell
MAY 3, 1947

Constantin Alajalov
MAY 10, 1947

Mead Schaeffer
MAY 17, 1947

John Falter
MAY 24, 1947

Albert Staehle
MAY 31, 1947

Constantin Alajalov
JUNE 7, 1947

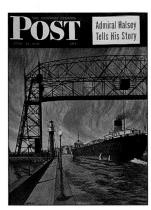

John Atherton
JUNE 14, 1947

Stevan Dohanos
JUNE 21, 1947

John Falter
JUNE 28, 1947

Stevan Dohanos
JULY 5, 1947

Mead Schaeffer
JULY 12, 1947

John Atherton
JULY 19, 1947

Constantin Alajalov
JULY 26, 1947

John Falter
AUGUST 2, 1947

Stevan Dohanos
AUGUST 9, 1947

Norman Rockwell
AUGUST 16, 1947

John Atherton
AUGUST 23, 1947

Norman Rockwell
AUGUST 30, 1947

Stevan Dohanos
SEPTEMBER 6, 1947

Alexander Brook
SEPTEMBER 13, 1947

Albert Staehle
SEPTEMBER 20, 1947

John Falter
SEPTEMBER 27, 1947

John Atherton
OCTOBER 4, 1947

Constantin Alajalov
OCTOBER 11, 1947

Stevan Dohanos
OCTOBER 18, 1947

Mead Schaeffer
OCTOBER 25, 1947

John Falter
NOVEMBER 1, 1947

Norman Rockwell
NOVEMBER 8, 1947

John Falter
NOVEMBER 15, 1947

John Atherton
NOVEMBER 22, 1947

Constantin Alajalov
NOVEMBER 29, 1947

Albert Staehle
DECEMBER 6, 1947

Stevan Dohanos
DECEMBER 13, 1947

Jack Welch
DECEMBER 20, 1947

Norman Rockwell
DECEMBER 27, 1947

John Falter
JANUARY 3, 1948

Mead Schaeffer
JANUARY 10, 1948

John Atherton
JANUARY 17, 1948

Norman Rockwell
JANUARY 24, 1948

Albert Staehle
JANUARY 31, 1948

John Falter
FEBRUARY 7, 1948

Stevan Dohanos
FEBRUARY 14, 1948

Constantin Alajalov
FEBRUARY 21, 1948

John Falter
FEBRUARY 28, 1948

Albert Staehle
MARCH 13, 1948

Stevan Dohanos
MARCH 20, 1948

John Falter
MARCH 27, 1948

Norman Rockwell
APRIL 3, 1948

John Atherton
APRIL 10, 1948

George Hughes
APRIL 17, 1948

Albert Staehle
APRIL 24, 1948

Stevan Dohanos
MAY 1, 1948

John Falter
MAY 8, 1948

Norman Rockwell
MAY 15, 1948

Constantin Alajalov
MAY 22, 1948

Mead Schaeffer
MAY 29, 1948

Stevan Dohanos
JUNE 5, 1948

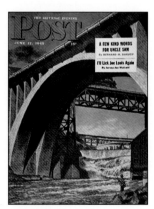

John Atherton
JUNE 12, 1948

John Falter
JUNE 19, 1948

Stevan Dohanos
JUNE 26, 1948

John Falter
JULY 3, 1948

Constantin Alajalov
JULY 10, 1948

John Atherton
JULY 17, 1948

John Falter
JULY 24, 1948

Stevan Dohanos
JULY 31, 1948

Constantin Alajalov
AUGUST 7, 1948

John Falter
AUGUST 14, 1948

Albert Staehle
AUGUST 21, 1948

Stevan Dohanos
AUGUST 28, 1948

Norman Rockwell
SEPTEMBER 4, 1948

George Hughes
SEPTEMBER 11, 1948

John Falter
SEPTEMBER 18, 1948

George Hughes
SEPTEMBER 25, 1948

Stevan Dohanos
OCTOBER 2, 1948

Mead Schaeffer
OCTOBER 9, 1948

George Hughes
OCTOBER 16, 1948

Constantin Alajalov
OCTOBER 23, 1948

Norman Rockwell
OCTOBER 30, 1948

John Atherton
NOVEMBER 6, 1948

Stevan Dohanos
NOVEMBER 13, 1948

John Falter
NOVEMBER 20, 1948

Constantin Alajalov
NOVEMBER 27, 1948

Stevan Dohanos
DECEMBER 4, 1948

George Hughes
DECEMBER 11, 1948

John Falter
DECEMBER 18, 1948

Norman Rockwell
DECEMBER 25, 1948

Constantin Alajalov
JANUARY 1, 1949

Stevan Dohanos
JANUARY 8, 1949

John Atherton
JANUARY 15, 1949

George Hughes
JANUARY 22, 1949

Albert Staehle
JANUARY 29, 1949

John Falter
FEBRUARY 5, 1949

Constantin Alajalov
FEBRUARY 12, 1949

Jack Welch
FEBRUARY 19, 1949

John Falter
FEBRUARY 26, 1949

Stevan Dohanos
MARCH 5, 1949

Constantin Alajalov
MARCH 12, 1949

Norman Rockwell
MARCH 19, 1949

John Falter
MARCH 26, 1949

Albert Staehle
APRIL 2, 1949

Constantin Alajalov
APRIL 9, 1949

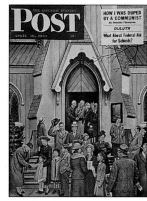

Stevan Dohanos
APRIL 16, 1949

John Falter
APRIL 30, 1949

Constantin Alajalov
MAY 7, 1949

Stevan Dohanos
MAY 14, 1949

George Hughes
MAY 21, 1949

Mead Schaeffer
MAY 28, 1949

John Falter
JUNE 4, 1949

Stevan Dohanos
JUNE 11, 1949

Albert Staehle
JUNE 18, 1949

Mead Schaeffer
JUNE 25, 1949

Stevan Dohanos
JULY 2, 1949

Norman Rockwell
JULY 9, 1949

Jack Welch
JULY 16, 1949

Austin Briggs
JULY 23, 1949

John Clymer
JULY 30, 1949

George Hughes
AUGUST 6, 1949

John Falter
AUGUST 13, 1949

Stevan Dohanos
AUGUST 20, 1949

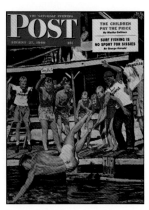

Austin Briggs
AUGUST 27, 1949

George Hughes
SEPTEMBER 3, 1949

Thornton Utz
SEPTEMBER 10, 1949

Amos Sewell
SEPTEMBER 17, 1949

Norman Rockwell
SEPTEMBER 24, 1949

Constantin Alajalov
OCTOBER 1, 1949

John Clymer
OCTOBER 8, 1949

Thornton Utz
OCTOBER 15, 1949

Stevan Dohanos
OCTOBER 22, 1949

Albert Staehle
OCTOBER 29, 1949

Norman Rockwell
NOVEMBER 5, 1949

Stevan Dohanos
NOVEMBER 12, 1949

George Hughes
NOVEMBER 19, 1949

Stevan Dohanos
NOVEMBER 26, 1949

John Falter
DECEMBER 3, 1949

Constantin Alajalov
DECEMBER 10, 1949

John Clymer
DECEMBER 17, 1949

George Hughes
DECEMBER 24, 1949

Constantin Alajalov
DECEMBER 31, 1949

Norman Rockwell
NOVEMBER 24, 1951

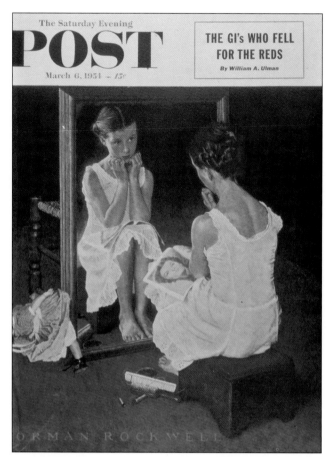

Norman Rockwell
MARCH 6, 1954

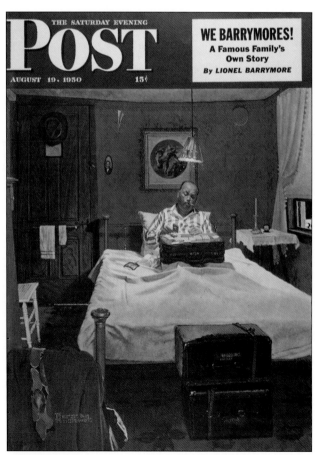

Norman Rockwell
AUGUST 19, 1950

Norman Rockwell
SEPTEMBER 25, 1954

CHAPTER 6

THE FIFTIES

In the 1950s, the covers of the *Saturday Evening Post* succeeded as never before in representing the American way of life. Ben Hibbs maintained the policy of featuring the work of a small number of artists, some of whom did ten or more cover illustrations each year. Constantin Alajalov, John Clymer, Stevan Dohanos, John Falter, George Hughes, Amos Sewell, Thornton Utz, and of course Norman Rockwell continued the work they had previously done for the magazine. As the decade progressed, they were joined by Ben Kimberly Prins and Richard (Dick) Sargent; all told, these ten men produced more than 450 covers during these years. Their styles and their approaches were various, but the principal subject matter for each of them was America and the American people.

The work of Norman Rockwell had by this time become inextricably bound up with the idea and the image of the *Post*. During the fifties, in more than forty covers, Rockwell continued to explore his own vision of America, partly nostalgic, partly humorous, always keenly realized. In "Saying Grace," an elderly woman and a young boy bow their heads in prayer, astonishing the other patrons at a cheap restaurant (November 24, 1951; page 214, top left). "Solitaire" depicts the interior of a shabby hotel, with the salesman's cases on the floor and the salesman in bed, his suitcase on his lap, playing a lonely game of solitaire (August 19, 1950; page 214, bottom left).

Rockwell's cover paintings are filled with details that enhance both the implied narrative and the mood. "Breaking Home Ties" teeters on the edge of sentimentalism, but the rooting in detail saves it. A working man, no doubt a farmer, sits in his work clothes by his son. The son is dressed in a suit, and his fancy red-and-white tie and socks match the colors of the State U. banner on his suitcase. The father's face is unreadable; the son's is filled with expectation. The collie, resting his head on the boy's leg, expresses the sadness restrained in the face of the father (September 25, 1954; page 214, bottom right). In "Girl and the Mirror," the mirror reflects a sad and thoughtful girl, dressed in her slip. She has cast her doll aside and—as the comb and brush and lipstick on the floor make clear—has entered adolescence, fixing her hair and experimenting with lipstick. On her lap is a movie magazine open to a photograph of Jane Russell. As the girl stares into the mirror, we read her intense disappointment in her own features. Nevertheless, Rockwell has painted a very pretty little girl (March 6, 1954; page 214, top right).

Rockwell took on a new kind of cover illustration for the *Post* in 1952. For the first time in many years, the magazine decided to feature portraiture, and it did so in conjunction with the presidential election. For the October 11, 1952, cover, Rockwell painted the head of the Republican candidate, Dwight D. Eisenhower. For the 1956 election, the *Post* was more evenhanded; that year Rockwell did a portrait of Adlai Stevenson, the Democratic contender, as well as a second portrait of Eisenhower (October 6 and 13; page 217, top right and left). For many years, Rockwell continued to paint portraits of presidential candidates for the cover of the *Post*.

Rockwell also painted Bob Hope's portrait, for the February 13, 1954, cover, of the issue that introduced the beginning of Hope's memoirs. And for June 28, 1958, he did an unusual portrait of the jockey Eddie Arcaro. The cover is known by the title "Weighing In"; we see the jockey on the scale, his saddle in his hands, while a much larger man in dark glasses hovers over him, making notes on his racing form. The cover is something of a tour de force, because, while Rockwell comments on horse racing, he also manages to present us with a portrait of the famous Arcaro (page 217, bottom left).

The 1950s, of course, brought prosperity to America, and it is this sense of well-being, security, and contentment that the covers of the *Post* reflect. Although the articles inside the magazine, and the announcement of special titles on the cover, kept up a constant alarm over Communism abroad and Communists at home, Cold War anxiety was absent from the cover art. In its place were familiar cover subjects: western vistas, rural panoramas, and urban scenes, but along with these was a new and pre-

Norman Rockwell
OCTOBER 13, 1956

Norman Rockwell
OCTOBER 6, 1956

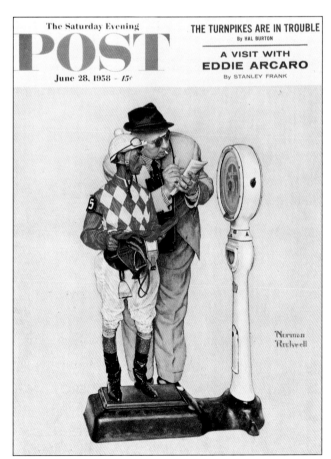

Norman Rockwell
JUNE 28, 1958

Norman Rockwell
SEPTEMBER 20, 1958

dominating fascination with suburbia and the nuclear family.

Certainly, the emphasis on the West and the fondness for the family farm were, by 1950, signs of nostalgia. In an increasingly urban and, especially, suburban society, these landscape paintings represented more an ideal, even a lost ideal, than a current reality. Beyond that, and more realistically, a more prosperous and mobile America was now able to enter these pristine landscapes on vacation. Some of the illustrators who painted rural and western America peopled their vistas with figures who suggested the accessibility of these worlds.

John Clymer specialized in western landscapes. Typically, he placed small figures in the foreground of his panoramic paintings, at once humanizing his landscapes and leaving the majority of the space available for nature painting. Sometimes his figures belong to the landscape, in the sense that they are seen working there. Examples include herding horses in Wyoming and a roundup on the Yakima River (September 13, 1952; May 10, 1958). But more often his figures have an ambiguous relation to the land; they may simply be visitors. These figures walk or hike, along a Colorado creek, in the Olympic Mountains, through an aspen forest, or on Mount Rainier (October 13, 1951; May 31 and October 18, 1952; July 17, 1954; see page 226, top). Sometimes they ride horses, through an apple orchard or an autumn woodland (May 6, 1950; October 20, 1956). Clymer frequently placed children in his paintings, a boy feeding a fawn or little girls feeding, on one cover, a chipmunk, and on another, a deer (May 27, 1950; May 16, 1953; August 25, 1956). In all cases the figures are dwarfed by the grandeur of the landscape, the beauty of the American West.

John Philips Falter, a master of many subjects, painted scenes of American farm life. Often members of farm families are included, though they are never shown engaged in farm work. The activities of the families, and particularly of the children, are those appropriate to all American families. Through the conjunction of the farm landscape and these typical activities, Falter created a kind of national unity between rural and suburban America. He painted one farm family playing a game of baseball, another enjoying a picnic by a lake. Farm children fly a kite in the middle of a field (September 2, 1950; August 18, 1951; March 18, 1950; see page 226, bottom). So broadly American were these activities that Falter could readily transplant them from the country to the suburbs; thus, his farm family's baseball game is replayed a few years later in the suburbs, where he paints a Little League home run (July 6, 1957).

But neither the West nor the farm was the primary setting for *Post* covers. The *Post*, like America, had moved to the suburbs. And if the automobile was the prime factor in that move, the *Post* recognized this in covers that examined from a variety of viewpoints America's love affair with the car. Stevan Dohanos painted a cover of teenage boys at work on a jalopy of their own and one of a young boy extravagantly admiring a fancy motorbike, and Amos Sewell did another of teenagers checking out a sporty car as a nervous dealer looks on (May 20, 1950—page 220, bottom right; April 7, 1951; December 8, 1956). In a later cover, Dohanos turned to the frustration of motoring: a Model T Ford holds up a line of irritated motorists as it struggles up a steep hill. The same irritation is apparent in the motorists who are forced to wait at a tollgate while a woman driver searches for change to pay the toll (October 9, 1954; April 7, 1956). Women drivers remained a fruitful stereotype for *Post* illustrators:

Thornton Utz painted one who has managed to block a trolley car. Utz also drew the downside of a drive in the country: the picturesque country road is blocked with traffic (April 1, 1950; May 30, 1959). George Hughes painted a different version of the bleaker side of motoring with a couple on a throughway: they have missed their exit and, as a sign informs them, it is thirty-one miles to the next one (June 15, 1957).

Suburban life is marked not only by cars but by school buses and commuter trains as well. Utz treated commuting on the June 28, 1952, cover, drawn in two horizontal panels: the first shows a well-dressed man, whose wife has driven him to the station, walk off filled with energy to catch his train; in the second, the same man returns home, tired and rumpled. Wives not only drove their husbands to the train, they were also responsible for dealing with male absentmindedness. Utz did a cover of a woman in nightgown and bathrobe, racing from her car after the departing commuter train, her husband's briefcase in her hand (February 2, 1957; page 221, bottom left). Mothers had the same responsibilities for their children. A Hughes cover for March 5, 1955, shows a woman racing out of her house after the school bus; she is carrying the forgotten lunchbox. An Amos Sewell cover gives Mom a break: through the picture window we see the kids troop to the school bus; inside Mom has relaxed on the sofa with coffee and the newspaper. School has begun (September 12, 1959).

Herbert Hoover had once promised a car in every garage; the *Post* covers seemed more interested in the premise that there would be a garage, and a driveway, for every car. Driveways had to be shoveled, as Earl Mayan recorded in a two-panel cover: on the top a man shovels, on the bottom the snowplow passes and blocks the drive with a mountain of snow (December 18, 1954; page 221, top left). In a Hughes cover, Father has returned to the suburbs after his day's work; the garage door is open but he can't park the car—the driveway is littered with toys (December 12, 1953). Falter painted two anxious parents in their driveway, for on the roof of the garage is their son, prepared to attempt flight (June 20, 1953). In a Dohanos cover, for May 22, 1954, the driveway and garage are again featured; in this painting the driveway is strewn with a few upset tables and chairs, and inside the garage is the birthday party that was suddenly interrupted by a rainstorm. The finest driveway cover is another Dohanos work: two women have backed out of their drives; unfortunately, they have backed into each other (August 4, 1956; page 223, top right).

The mobility of American life is noted as well in a number of covers that deal with moving day. Most often the treatment is comic. Dohanos made his subject the neighborhood dogs; from the edge of the front lawn a collection of dogs, none of them particularly fancy, watches as movers carry in furniture, but the object of their interest is a well-manicured poodle tied to the front porch (March 21, 1953). A cover by Hughes reveals a horrified woman, leaning out of her window as the movers carry a tuba and a drum set into the house next door (September 27, 1952). A less humorous, and perhaps more representative, painting also came from Hughes, who showed the moving van about to pull away and the neighborhood children surrounding a car and saying good-bye to their friends (September 29, 1956).

Suburban houses had yards as well as driveways—and yards, along with other suburban amenities, meant chores. Utz did a cover showing four backyards. In three of

Constantin Alajalov
JULY 28, 1951

Ben Kimberly Prins
SEPTEMBER 13, 1958

Richard Sargent
APRIL 12, 1958

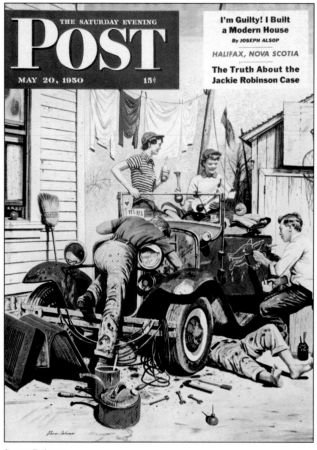

Stevan Dohanos
MAY 20, 1950

Earl Mayan
DECEMBER 18, 1954

John Falter
DECEMBER 24, 1955

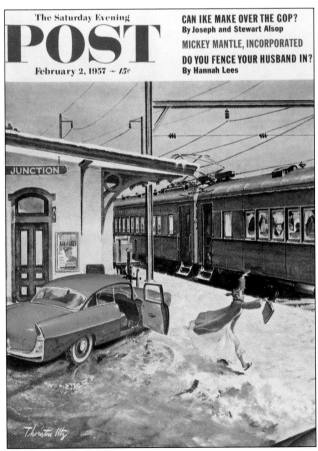

Thornton Utz
FEBRUARY 2, 1957

George Hughes
MARCH 5, 1955

them, young husbands are diligently gardening; the fourth has been paved over with stones and outfitted with a hammock, an umbrella, and some reading matter, and this householder is simply painting his backyard green (May 2, 1953). A few years later, Utz returned to this theme with a view of three backyards; again, in two of them men are hard at work, and in the third a happier man lounges and watches a baseball game on TV (May 18, 1957). Sewell provided another version of the contented father; he has fitted himself into the wading pool to the consternation of his small son and the family dog, for there is no room left for them (August 27, 1955). But Sewell's dads were not all so comfortable. The June 16, 1956, cover shows one struggling to erect a jungle gym. A Sargent cover hovers between work and leisure. The suburban husband has a tree to plant, but for the moment he is content to rest in the shade of the tree he will plant—a little later (April 12, 1958; page 220, bottom left). Hughes, too, painted a cover about tree planting, but in this case the wife is in charge. She cannot decide where the new tree should go, and the harassed gardener has already dug four holes (April 9, 1955).

Gender stereotyping offered abundant opportunities for cover illustrators to delineate American life in the 1950s. The man of the family not only did the yard work, he is often also shown as loaded down, burdened with the abundant, even excessive, family gear. In one example, he and his wife have taken the new baby to visit the grandparents; in this Sewell cover, for August 3, 1957, the wife stands at the top of the porch with her parents, holding the baby, while the husband struggles at the foot of the steps with a mountain of baby equipment. Vacations brought the same burdens. In Hughes's version the family is just arriving:

Mom is seen on the porch of the small cabin, and the children rush off to the water; Dad, meanwhile, is near the car, hefting three suitcases (August 11, 1956). Dohanos painted the end of vacation: Dad surveys the welter of suitcases and sports equipment he is supposed to fit into the trunk of the car (September 8, 1956). And Falter demonstrated that the chores do not end with the vacation. On his August 23, 1952, cover the family has just returned home; once again, Dad is carrying the bags, but now he surveys the overgrown lawn. During the vacation, to be sure, it was Mom who ended up stuck with all the work. Another Dohanos cover places the viewer behind a woman at the sink as she does the dishes; through the window we see the family at the beach, at play, and at rest (July 19, 1952).

The man of the family worried about money, while his wife, and sometimes his children, enjoyed prosperity without a thought of the cost. Alajalov painted a man and wife moving into a French hotel room; as the wife looks out the window at the scene below, the husband investigates the price chart on the back of the door (July 14, 1956). Hughes did a cover of a family investigating a model home; again the father looks at the card that explains the price (September 28, 1957). And the April 18, 1959, cover, by Kurt Ard, shows a teenaged girl trying on a dress for the prom; Mom is delighted at the effect, but Dad is leaning over for a look at the price tag. At the grocery store, Mom could run out of money; a cover by Hughes shows a couple at the check-out counter—the embarrassed wife holds out her hand to her husband, who reaches for his wallet (July 21, 1951).

Most of the women on the covers of the 1950s *Post* were, of course, homemakers, but they were more typically depicted

Amos Sewell
SEPTEMBER 12, 1959

Stevan Dohanos
AUGUST 4, 1956

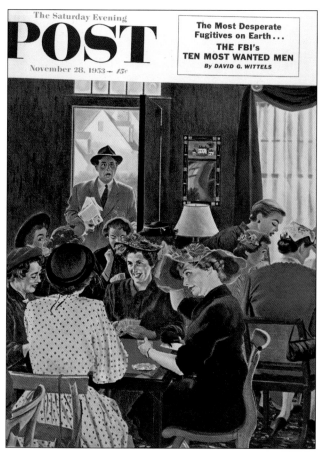

George Hughes
NOVEMBER 28, 1953

Thornton Utz
JANUARY 25, 1958

223

bridge players. There were numerous variations on this theme. Hughes depicted the unhappy husband, home from work, to find his house filled with bridge-playing women. Another Hughes bridge party is interrupted by a neighborhood gossip, whose interminable conversation with the hostess holds up the game (November 28, 1953—page 223, bottom left; May 12, 1951). Sargent placed the bridge game in the background, seen through an open door; in the foreground, a boy plunders the elegant desserts set out for the women (December 20, 1952).

There were other kinds of parties as well, as the *Post* artists recorded. There were barbecues, with the husband at the grill. Alajalov painted him in the rain, working under a small umbrella while the guests, dry on the porch, wait impatiently (July 28, 1951; page 220, top left). And Ben Prins showed him alone in the yard, far from the guests on the patio, but surrounded by all the dogs in the neighborhood (September 13, 1958; page 220, top right). Indoor parties, too, were subject to the predation of dogs—and small boys. Typically, these covers are designed so that the foray occurs in the foreground, with the party seen only through a doorway behind. Dohanos painted a small boy emptying all the party guests' purses (November 22, 1952). Utz carried this idea out in a cover that showed a child at play in the bedroom amid the coats and hats of the guests enjoying themselves in the living room (January 25, 1958; page 223, bottom right). A Sewell cover catches young boys plundering the party food in the refrigerator, and Sargent painted the family dog climbing eagerly onto a loaded buffet table (February 19, 1955). A variation on this theme on the November 24, 1956, cover, by Prins, depicts a bridge game for couples, again seen through

an open door; it is interrupted when one of the four infants asleep in carriers in the bedroom begins to howl.

These party scenes, with their narrative distributed between foreground and background, were only one way in which *Post* cover artists of the period often divided their paintings up so as to develop a series of stages in their narrative. A number of covers from these years were split into two or three horizontal sections, and sometimes even more. In a few instances as many as nine separate panels were used to complete the story. Dick Sargent did a number of split-level covers. In one he told the story of an electric train. On the top, the father sees his son play with a small wooden train. In the middle, Father purchases a fine electric train. And at the bottom, with the train set up on the floor, the son plays with the packing boxes (December 19, 1953). A Sargent cover for March 20, 1954, was divided into quarters to tell its story: the boss yells at an employee, the employee returns home and yells at his wife, the wife yells at their little son, and the son yells at the cat.

Utz, too, employed this method of multiple frames. In one three-level cover, a pillow fight erupts on the top; in the center Dad climbs the stairs, but the boys hear him; in the final picture, Dad enters the bedroom to find two angelic boys asleep (November 19, 1955). In another, Utz painted a man fishing on a bridge; he is, at first, alone on the left, but he—and not the crowd on the right—lands a fish. In the center, the crowd rushes to the left and the man moves to the right side of the bridge. And on the bottom we find that the lone man has again been successful (August 8, 1959). In a nine-frame cover for May 12, 1956, Utz traced the day of a family man whose wife is in the hospital about to give birth. He rises, cooks, cleans, goes to work, markets, tends to the children, visits the hospital, and finds his wife has had twins. Alajalov, too, worked with multiple images, as well as with his particular brand of irony. One two-level cover showed a wife on the top, looking romantically out of the bedroom window at the moon; below, her husband is happily engaged in his basement workshop (May 8, 1954). Another cover, in nine frames, comments on marriage. We see, in this order, a woman at her desk, her introduction to a man, a series of dates at the theater, dancing, the beach, then the wedding, the honeymoon, the return home, and, at the end, the woman back at her desk—married but still working (June 1, 1957).

Alajalov's wry statements notwithstanding, and the comic frustrations of suburban life aside, the *Post* covers of the fifties celebrated marriage, the American family, and the prosperous new life of the postwar world. At no previous time had the covers of the magazine so explicitly detailed the physical world of America, the setting in which the figures were placed, the activities in which they were engaged, and the objects that they owned or coveted. The Christmas covers, formerly devoted to nostalgic or pious illustration, were now frequently domesticated. Alajalov did one for December 23, 1950, that showed the wife decorating one tree as her husband entered the front door with another. Dohanos painted a wife supervising her husband's attempt to fit the tree into the stand (December 22, 1951). In 1955, Falter painted three small children climbing down the stairs on Christmas morning; the tree and the presents are seen in the background (December 24; page 221, top right). The next year, Rockwell painted an astonished boy who has just discovered a Santa Claus suit in the bottom drawer of the bureau (December 29, 1956). In 1958, Prins did the Christmas cover, a three-level depic-

tion of the predation on the gifts (December 27). The celebration of materialism could go no further. In an abrupt about-face, the final Christmas cover of the decade announced "The Life of Christ" in sixteen color pages, "Painted by Italian Masters of the XI to XV Centuries." The cover reprinted an Adoration of the Magi (December 26, 1959; below).

But the work of Alajalov was truer to the times, again through the soft focus of his irony. The August 15, 1959, cover celebrated young love, Alajalov style. Nestled against a tree in the foreground, an engaged couple lies back romantically. The rest of the cover is filled with the representation of their dreams: a large suburban house, two cars, a swimming pool, three children—the youngest cared for by a nanny, a refrigerator, a washer and dryer, a television console, and all the smaller electrical appliances any couple in love could desire.

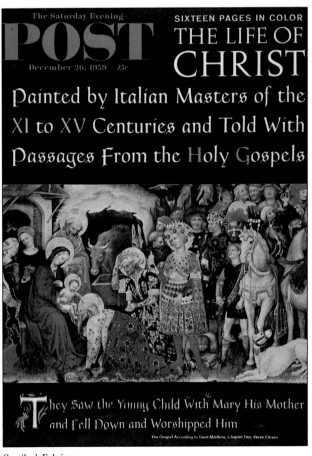

Gentile daFabriano
DECEMBER 26, 1959

John Clymer
MAY 31, 1952

John Clymer
JULY 17, 1954

John Falter
SEPTEMBER 2, 1950

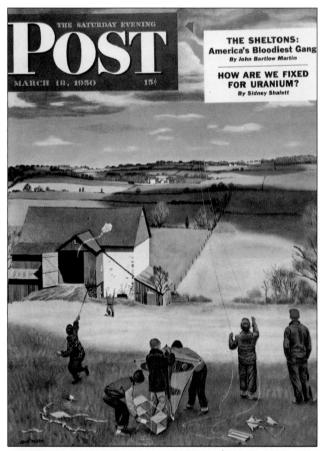

John Falter
MARCH 18, 1950

John Falter
JANUARY 7, 1950

John Atherton
JANUARY 14, 1950

M. Coburn Whitmore
JANUARY 21, 1950

George Hughes
JANUARY 28, 1950

Thornton Utz
FEBRUARY 4, 1950

John Falter
FEBRUARY 11, 1950

Jack Welch
FEBRUARY 18, 1950

George Hughes
FEBRUARY 25, 1950

Stevan Dohanos
MARCH 4, 1950

Amos Sewell
MARCH 11, 1950

Stevan Dohanos
MARCH 25, 1950

Thornton Utz
APRIL 1, 1950

Constantin Alajalov
APRIL 8, 1950

John Clymer
APRIL 15, 1950

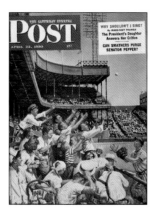

Stevan Dohanos
APRIL 22, 1950

Norman Rockwell
APRIL 29, 1950

227

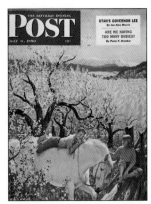

John Clymer
MAY 6, 1950

John Falter
MAY 13, 1950

John Clymer
MAY 27, 1950

M. Coburn Whitmore
JUNE 3, 1950

Stevan Dohanos
JUNE 10, 1950

George Hughes
JUNE 17, 1950

John Falter
JUNE 24, 1950

Stevan Dohanos
JULY 1, 1950

Amos Sewell
JULY 8, 1950

Constantin Alajalov
JULY 15, 1950

Stevan Dohanos
JULY 22, 1950

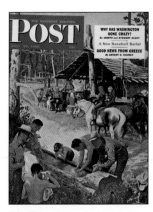

John Clymer
JULY 29, 1950

George Hughes
AUGUST 5, 1950

Mead Schaeffer
AUGUST 12, 1950

Stevan Dohanos
AUGUST 26, 1950

Amos Sewell
SEPTEMBER 9, 1950

228

Mead Schaeffer
SEPTEMBER 16, 1950

George Hughes
SEPTEMBER 23, 1950

Stevan Dohanos
SEPTEMBER 30, 1950

John Clymer
OCTOBER 7, 1950

Constantin Alajalov
OCTOBER 14, 1950

Norman Rockwell
OCTOBER 21, 1950

Jack Welch
OCTOBER 28, 1950

George Hughes
NOVEMBER 4, 1950

John Clymer
NOVEMBER 11, 1950

Norman Rockwell
NOVEMBER 18, 1950

Stevan Dohanos
NOVEMBER 25, 1950

George Hughes
DECEMBER 2, 1950

M. Coburn Whitmore
DECEMBER 9, 1950

Stevan Dohanos
DECEMBER 16, 1950

Constantin Alajalov
DECEMBER 23, 1950

John Clymer
DECEMBER 30, 1950

229

John Falter
JANUARY 6, 1951

George Hughes
JANUARY 13, 1951

John Atherton
JANUARY 20, 1951

John Clymer
JANUARY 27, 1951

Stevan Dohanos
FEBRUARY 3, 1951

George Hughes
FEBRUARY 10, 1951

John Clymer
FEBRUARY 17, 1951

Stevan Dohanos
FEBRUARY 24, 1951

John Falter
MARCH 3, 1951

Constantin Alajalov
MARCH 10, 1951

George Hughes
MARCH 17, 1951

Amos Sewell
MARCH 24, 1951

George Hughes
MARCH 31, 1951

Stevan Dohanos
APRIL 7, 1951

John Falter
APRIL 14, 1951

John Clymer
APRIL 21, 1951

Amos Sewell
APRIL 28, 1951

John Falter
MAY 5, 1951

George Hughes
MAY 12, 1951

Mead Schaeffer
MAY 19, 1951

Stevan Dohanos
MAY 26, 1951

Norman Rockwell
JUNE 2, 1951

John Clymer
JUNE 9, 1951

John Falter
JUNE 16, 1951

Amos Sewell
JUNE 23, 1951

Thornton Utz
JUNE 30, 1951

Stevan Dohanos
JULY 7, 1951

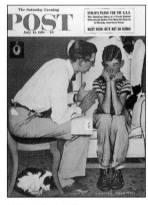

Norman Rockwell
JULY 14, 1951

George Hughes
JULY 21, 1951

John Clymer
AUGUST 4, 1951

Stevan Dohanos
AUGUST 11, 1951

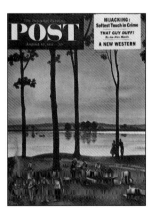

John Falter
AUGUST 18, 1951

Stevan Dohanos
AUGUST 25, 1951

George Hughes
SEPTEMBER 1, 1951

Jack Welch
SEPTEMBER 8, 1951

Mead Schaeffer
SEPTEMBER 15, 1951

Stevan Dohanos
SEPTEMBER 22, 1951

John Falter
SEPTEMBER 29, 1951

George Hughes
OCTOBER 6, 1951

John Clymer
OCTOBER 13, 1951

Thornton Utz
OCTOBER 20, 1951

Constantin Alajalov
OCTOBER 27, 1951

Amos Sewell
NOVEMBER 3, 1951

Stevan Dohanos
NOVEMBER 10, 1951

George Hughes
NOVEMBER 17, 1951

Mead Schaeffer
DECEMBER 1, 1951

John Falter
DECEMBER 8, 1951

Richard Sargent
DECEMBER 15, 1951

Stevan Dohanos
DECEMBER 22, 1951

George Hughes
DECEMBER 29, 1951

M. Coburn Whitmore
JANUARY 5, 1952

Constantin Alajalov
JANUARY 12, 1952

John Atherton
JANUARY 19, 1952

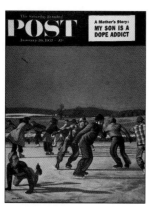

John Falter
JANUARY 26, 1952

Stevan Dohanos
FEBRUARY 2, 1952

Frank Kilker
FEBRUARY 9, 1952

Norman Rockwell
FEBRUARY 16, 1952

John Clymer
FEBRUARY 23, 1952

George Hughes
MARCH 1, 1952

Stevan Dohanos
MARCH 8, 1952

John Falter
MARCH 15, 1952

Amos Sewell
MARCH 22, 1952

Norman Rockwell
MARCH 29, 1952

Stevan Dohanos
APRIL 5, 1952

M. Coburn Whitmore
APRIL 12, 1952

Thornton Utz
APRIL 19, 1952

John Falter
APRIL 26, 1952

Richard Sargent
MAY 3, 1952

Stevan Dohanos
MAY 10, 1952

Mead Schaeffer
MAY 17, 1952

Norman Rockwell
MAY 24, 1952

Constantin Alajalov
JUNE 7, 1952

Amos Sewell
JUNE 14, 1952

George Hughes
JUNE 21, 1952

Thornton Utz
JUNE 28, 1952

John Falter
JULY 5, 1952

Mead Schaeffer
JULY 12, 1952

Stevan Dohanos
JULY 19, 1952

John Falter
JULY 26, 1952

George Hughes
AUGUST 2, 1952

Stevan Dohanos
AUGUST 9, 1952

Amos Sewell
AUGUST 16, 1952

John Falter
AUGUST 23, 1952

Norman Rockwell
AUGUST 30, 1952

George Hughes
SEPTEMBER 6, 1952

John Clymer
SEPTEMBER 13, 1952

Richard Sargent
SEPTEMBER 20, 1952

George Hughes
SEPTEMBER 27, 1952

Stevan Dohanos
OCTOBER 4, 1952

Norman Rockwell
OCTOBER 11, 1952

John Clymer
OCTOBER 18, 1952

George Hughes
OCTOBER 25, 1952

John Falter
NOVEMBER 1, 1952

Amos Sewell
NOVEMBER 8, 1952

John Clymer
NOVEMBER 15, 1952

Stevan Dohanos
NOVEMBER 22, 1952

George Hughes
NOVEMBER 29, 1952

John Falter
DECEMBER 6, 1952

Stevan Dohanos
DECEMBER 13, 1952

Richard Sargent
DECEMBER 20, 1952

Stevan Dohanos
DECEMBER 27, 1952

Norman Rockwell
JANUARY 3, 1953

John Falter
JANUARY 10, 1953

John Atherton
JANUARY 17, 1953

George Hughes
JANUARY 24, 1953

Stevan Dohanos
JANUARY 31, 1953

Jack Welch
FEBRUARY 7, 1953

George Hughes
FEBRUARY 14, 1953

Stevan Dohanos
FEBRUARY 21, 1953

Constantin Alajalov
FEBRUARY 28, 1953

Richard Sargent
MARCH 7, 1953

George Hughes
MARCH 14, 1953

236

Stevan Dohanos
MARCH 21, 1953

George Hughes
MARCH 28, 1953

Norman Rockwell
APRIL 4, 1953

Ben Kimberly Prins
APRIL 11, 1953

John Falter
APRIL 18, 1953

John Clymer
APRIL 25, 1953

Thornton Utz
MAY 2, 1953

Stevan Dohanos
MAY 9, 1953

John Clymer
MAY 16, 1953

Norman Rockwell
MAY 23, 1953

Mead Schaeffer
MAY 30, 1953

George Hughes
JUNE 6, 1953

Constantin Alajalov
JUNE 13, 1953

John Falter
JUNE 20, 1953

Amos Sewell
JUNE 27, 1953

Ben Kimberly Prins
JULY 4, 1953

John Falter
JULY 11, 1953

Richard Sargent
JULY 18, 1953

John Clymer
JULY 25, 1953

Stevan Dohanos
AUGUST 1, 1953

George Hughes
AUGUST 8, 1953

John Clymer
AUGUST 15, 1953

Norman Rockwell
AUGUST 22, 1953

Thornton Utz
AUGUST 29, 1953

Amos Sewell
SEPTEMBER 5, 1953

Constantin Alajalov
SEPTEMBER 12, 1953

Stevan Dohanos
SEPTEMBER 19, 1953

George Hughes
SEPTEMBER 26, 1953

Amos Sewell
OCTOBER 3, 1953

Ben Kimberly Prins
OCTOBER 10, 1953

John Falter
OCTOBER 17, 1953

Thornton Utz
OCTOBER 24, 1953

John Clymer
OCTOBER 31, 1953

Constantin Alajalov
NOVEMBER 7, 1953

Stevan Dohanos
NOVEMBER 14, 1953

Richard Sargent
NOVEMBER 21, 1953

Stevan Dohanos
DECEMBER 5, 1953

George Hughes
DECEMBER 12, 1953

Richard Sargent
DECEMBER 19, 1953

Mead Schaeffer
DECEMBER 26, 1953

Thornton Utz
JANUARY 2, 1954

Norman Rockwell
JANUARY 9, 1954

John Atherton
JANUARY 16, 1954

John Clymer
JANUARY 23, 1954

Stevan Dohanos
JANUARY 30, 1954

George Hughes
FEBRUARY 6, 1954

Norman Rockwell
FEBRUARY 13, 1954

Amos Sewell
FEBRUARY 20, 1954

Stevan Dohanos
FEBRUARY 27, 1954

George Hughes
MARCH 13, 1954

Richard Sargent
MARCH 20, 1954

Stevan Dohanos
MARCH 27, 1954

Ben Kimberly Prins
APRIL 3, 1954

Thornton Utz
APRIL 10, 1954

Norman Rockwell
APRIL 17, 1954

Amos Sewell
APRIL 24, 1954

John Falter
MAY 1, 1954

Constantin Alajalov
MAY 8, 1954

George Hughes
MAY 15, 1954

Stevan Dohanos
MAY 22, 1954

John Clymer
MAY 29, 1954

John Falter
JUNE 5, 1954

George Hughes
JUNE 12, 1954

Richard Sargent
JUNE 19, 1954

Stevan Dohanos
JUNE 26, 1954

George Hughes
JULY 3, 1954

Ben Kimberly Prins
JULY 10, 1954

George Hughes
JULY 24, 1954

Stevan Dohanos
JULY 31, 1954

Thornton Utz
AUGUST 7, 1954

John Falter
AUGUST 14, 1954

Norman Rockwell
AUGUST 21, 1954

George Hughes
AUGUST 28, 1954

Constantin Alajalov
SEPTEMBER 4, 1954

Stevan Dohanos
SEPTEMBER 11, 1954

John Clymer
SEPTEMBER 18, 1954

Thornton Utz
OCTOBER 2, 1954

Stevan Dohanos
OCTOBER 9, 1954

John Clymer
OCTOBER 16, 1954

John Falter
OCTOBER 23, 1954

Stevan Dohanos
OCTOBER 30, 1954

Richard Sargent
NOVEMBER 6, 1954

Constantin Alajalov
NOVEMBER 13, 1954

Thornton Utz
NOVEMBER 20, 1954

George Hughes
NOVEMBER 27, 1954

John Clymer
DECEMBER 4, 1954

Amos Sewell
DECEMBER 11, 1954

George Hughes
DECEMBER 25, 1954

Stevan Dohanos
JANUARY 1, 1955

John Falter
JANUARY 8, 1955

John Atherton
JANUARY 15, 1955

John Clymer
JANUARY 22, 1955

Amos Sewell
JANUARY 29, 1955

Richard Sargent
FEBRUARY 5, 1955

Ben Kimberly Prins
FEBRUARY 12, 1955

Amos Sewell
FEBRUARY 19, 1955

Stevan Dohanos
FEBRUARY 26, 1955

Norman Rockwell
MARCH 12, 1955

Stevan Dohanos
MARCH 19, 1955

John Falter
MARCH 26, 1955

Richard Sargent
APRIL 2, 1955

George Hughes
APRIL 9, 1955

Norman Rockwell
APRIL 16, 1955

Earl Mayan
APRIL 23, 1955

Stevan Dohanos
APRIL 30, 1955

John Clymer
MAY 7, 1955

George Hughes
MAY 14, 1955

Stevan Dohanos
MAY 21, 1955

John Falter
MAY 28, 1955

Richard Sargent
JUNE 4, 1955

Norman Rockwell
JUNE 11, 1955

Thornton Utz
JUNE 18, 1955

John Clymer
JUNE 25, 1955

George Hughes
JULY 2, 1955

Amos Sewell
JULY 9, 1955

John Clymer
JULY 16, 1955

Thornton Utz
JULY 23, 1955

Constantin Alajalov
JULY 30, 1955

John Falter
AUGUST 6, 1955

John Clymer
AUGUST 13, 1955

Norman Rockwell
AUGUST 20, 1955

Amos Sewell
AUGUST 27, 1955

Stevan Dohanos
SEPTEMBER 3, 1955

George Hughes
SEPTEMBER 10, 1955

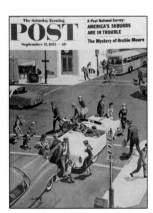

Thornton Utz
SEPTEMBER 17, 1955

George Hughes
SEPTEMBER 24, 1955

Richard Sargent
OCTOBER 1, 1955

John Clymer
OCTOBER 8, 1955

Constantin Alajalov
OCTOBER 15, 1955

George Hughes
OCTOBER 22, 1955

M. Coburn Whitmore
OCTOBER 29, 1955

John Falter
NOVEMBER 5, 1955

Ben Kimberly Prins
NOVEMBER 12, 1955

Thornton Utz
NOVEMBER 19, 1955

John Clymer
NOVEMBER 26, 1955

John Falter
DECEMBER 3, 1955

Richard Sargent
DECEMBER 10, 1955

John Clymer
DECEMBER 17, 1955

George Hughes
DECEMBER 31, 1955

George Hughes
JANUARY 7, 1956

Stevan Dohanos
JANUARY 14, 1956

Stanley Meltzoff
JANUARY 21, 1956

Amos Sewell
JANUARY 28, 1956

John Clymer
FEBRUARY 4, 1956

Richard Sargent
FEBRUARY 11, 1956

George Hughes
FEBRUARY 18, 1956

Richard Sargent
FEBRUARY 25, 1956

Stevan Dohanos
MARCH 3, 1956

John Clymer
MARCH 10, 1956

Norman Rockwell
MARCH 17, 1956

George Hughes
MARCH 24, 1956

Amos Sewell
MARCH 31, 1956

Stevan Dohanos
APRIL 7, 1956

Richard Sargent
APRIL 14, 1956

John Falter
APRIL 21, 1956

Earl Mayan
APRIL 28, 1956

John Clymer
MAY 5, 1956

Thornton Utz
MAY 12, 1956

Norman Rockwell
MAY 19, 1956

John Falter
MAY 26, 1956

246

Earl Mayan
JUNE 2, 1956

Ben Kimberly Prins
JUNE 9, 1956

Amos Sewell
JUNE 16, 1956

John Clymer
JUNE 23, 1956

John Falter
JUNE 30, 1956

George Hughes
JULY 7, 1956

Constantin Alajalov
JULY 14, 1956

John Falter
JULY 21, 1956

Amos Sewell
JULY 28, 1956

George Hughes
AUGUST 11, 1956

Constantin Alajalov
AUGUST 18, 1956

John Clymer
AUGUST 25, 1956

Richard Sargent
SEPTEMBER 1, 1956

Stevan Dohanos
SEPTEMBER 8, 1956

Thornton Utz
SEPTEMBER 15, 1956

Ben Kimberly Prins
SEPTEMBER 22, 1956

George Hughes
SEPTEMBER 29, 1956

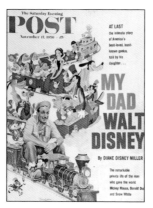

John Clymer
OCTOBER 20, 1956

John Falter
OCTOBER 27, 1956

George Hughes
NOVEMBER 3, 1956

Constantin Alajalov
NOVEMBER 10, 1956

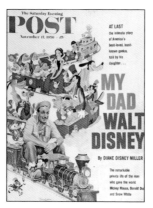

Gustaf Tenggren
NOVEMBER 17, 1956

Ben Kimberly Prins
NOVEMBER 24, 1956

John Falter
DECEMBER 1, 1956

Amos Sewell
DECEMBER 8, 1956

George Hughes
DECEMBER 15, 1956

John Clymer
DECEMBER 22, 1956

Norman Rockwell
DECEMBER 29, 1956

Richard Sargent
JANUARY 5, 1957

Stevan Dohanos
JANUARY 12, 1957

Stanley Meltzoff
JANUARY 19, 1957

Amos Sewell
JANUARY 26, 1957

George Hughes
FEBRUARY 9, 1957

Stevan Dohanos
FEBRUARY 16, 1957

Constantin Alajalov
FEBRUARY 23, 1957

Norman Rockwell
MARCH 2, 1957

Ben Kimberly Prins
MARCH 9, 1957

Thornton Utz
MARCH 16, 1957

John Clymer
MARCH 23, 1957

George Hughes
MARCH 30, 1957

Ben Kimberly Prins
APRIL 6, 1957

Constantin Alajalov
APRIL 13, 1957

Earl Mayan
APRIL 20, 1957

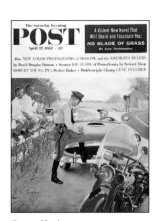

George Hughes
APRIL 27, 1957

John Falter
MAY 4, 1957

Richard Sargent
MAY 11, 1957

Thornton Utz
MAY 18, 1957

Norman Rockwell
MAY 25, 1957

Constantin Alajalov
JUNE 1, 1957

George Hughes
JUNE 8, 1957

George Hughes
JUNE 15, 1957

John Clymer
JUNE 22, 1957

Norman Rockwell
JUNE 29, 1957

John Falter
JULY 6, 1957

Stevan Dohanos
JULY 13, 1957

George Hughes
JULY 20, 1957

John Clymer
JULY 27, 1957

Amos Sewell
AUGUST 3, 1957

Ben Kimberly Prins
AUGUST 10, 1957

Thornton Utz
AUGUST 17, 1957

Earl Mayan
AUGUST 24, 1957

Constantin Alajalov
AUGUST 31, 1957

Norman Rockwell
SEPTEMBER 7, 1957

D. Bleitz
SEPTEMBER 14, 1957

John Clymer
SEPTEMBER 21, 1957

George Hughes
SEPTEMBER 28, 1957

Richard Sargent
OCTOBER 5, 1957

John Falter
OCTOBER 12, 1957

Kurt Ard
OCTOBER 19, 1957

John Clymer
OCTOBER 26, 1957

George Hughes
NOVEMBER 2, 1957

John Falter
NOVEMBER 9, 1957

John Falter
NOVEMBER 16, 1957

George Hughes
NOVEMBER 23, 1957

Norman Rockwell
NOVEMBER 30, 1957

Richard Sargent
DECEMBER 7, 1957

Ben Kimberly Prins
DECEMBER 14, 1957

John Clymer
DECEMBER 21, 1957

John Falter
DECEMBER 28, 1957

Ben Kimberly Prins
JANUARY 4, 1958

John Falter
JANUARY 11, 1958

Stanley Meltzoff
JANUARY 18, 1958

John Clymer
FEBRUARY 1, 1958

George Hughes
FEBRUARY 8, 1958

Amos Sewell
FEBRUARY 15, 1958

Kurt Ard
FEBRUARY 22, 1958

George Hughes
MARCH 1, 1958

Amos Sewell
MARCH 8, 1958

Norman Rockwell
MARCH 15, 1958

M. Coburn Whitmore
MARCH 22, 1958

Ben Kimberly Prins
MARCH 29, 1958

Gustaf Tenggren
APRIL 5, 1958

John Falter
APRIL 19, 1958

George Hughes
APRIL 26, 1958

Thornton Utz
MAY 3, 1958

John Clymer
MAY 10, 1958

Ben Kimberly Prins
MAY 17, 1958

E. Melbourne Brindle
MAY 24, 1958

Constantin Alajalov
MAY 31, 1958

George Hughes
JUNE 7, 1958

Earl Mayan
JUNE 14, 1958

John Falter
JUNE 21, 1958

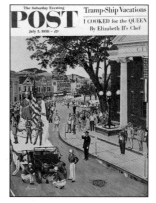

Ben Kimberly Prins
JULY 5, 1958

Amos Sewell
JULY 12, 1958

Thornton Utz
JULY 19, 1958

Ben Kimberly Prins
JULY 26, 1958

Constantin Alajalov
AUGUST 2, 1958

Earl Mayan
AUGUST 9, 1958

Kurt Ard
AUGUST 16, 1958

Thornton Utz
AUGUST 23, 1958

Norman Rockwell
AUGUST 30, 1958

Thornton Utz
SEPTEMBER 6, 1958

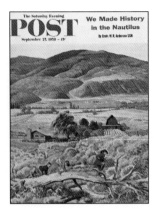

John Clymer
SEPTEMBER 27, 1958

Ben Kimberly Prins
OCTOBER 4, 1958

Stevan Dohanos
OCTOBER 11, 1958

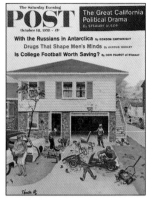

Thornton Utz
OCTOBER 18, 1958

John Clymer
OCTOBER 25, 1958

John Falter
NOVEMBER 1, 1958

Norman Rockwell
NOVEMBER 8, 1958

Kurt Ard
NOVEMBER 15, 1958

George Hughes
NOVEMBER 22, 1958

Amos Sewell
NOVEMBER 29, 1958

George Hughes
DECEMBER 6, 1958

John Clymer
DECEMBER 13, 1958

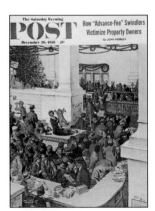

Thornton Utz
DECEMBER 20, 1958

Ben Kimberly Prins
DECEMBER 27, 1958

Constantin Alajalov
JANUARY 3, 1959

George Hughes
JANUARY 10, 1959

Stanley Meltzoff
JANUARY 17, 1959

John Falter
JANUARY 24, 1959

George Hughes
JANUARY 31, 1959

Richard Sargent
FEBRUARY 7, 1959

Norman Rockwell
FEBRUARY 14, 1959

John Falter
FEBRUARY 21, 1959

George Hughes
FEBRUARY 28, 1959

Richard Sargent
MARCH 7, 1959

Kurt Ard
MARCH 14, 1959

Constantin Alajalov
MARCH 21, 1959

George Hughes
MARCH 28, 1959

John Falter
APRIL 4, 1959

Richard Sargent
APRIL 11, 1959

Kurt Ard
APRIL 18, 1959

Earl Mayan
APRIL 25, 1959

Constantin Alajalov
MAY 2, 1959

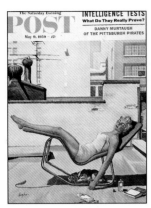

George Hughes
MAY 9, 1959

Norman Rockwell
MAY 16, 1959

John Clymer
MAY 23, 1959

Thornton Utz
MAY 30, 1959

Norman Rockwell
JUNE 6, 1959

John Clymer
JUNE 13, 1959

John Falter
JUNE 20, 1959

Amos Sewell
JUNE 27, 1959

Thornton Utz
JULY 4, 1959

Richard Sargent
JULY 11, 1959

John Falter
JULY 18, 1959

John Clymer
JULY 25, 1959

James W. Williamson
AUGUST 1, 1959

Thornton Utz
AUGUST 8, 1959

Constantin Alajalov
AUGUST 15, 1959

Richard Sargent
AUGUST 22, 1959

John Clymer
AUGUST 29, 1959

John Falter
SEPTEMBER 5, 1959

Constantin Alajalov
SEPTEMBER 19, 1959

Kurt Ard
SEPTEMBER 26, 1959

George Hughes
OCTOBER 3, 1959

John Clymer
OCTOBER 10, 1959

Richard Sargent
OCTOBER 17, 1959

Norman Rockwell
OCTOBER 24, 1959

Ben Kimberly Prins
OCTOBER 31, 1959

George Hughes
NOVEMBER 7, 1959

John Clymer
NOVEMBER 14, 1959

Thornton Utz
NOVEMBER 21, 1959

John Clymer
NOVEMBER 28, 1959

Constantin Alajalov
DECEMBER 5, 1959

Amos Sewell
DECEMBER 12, 1959

Richard Sargent
DECEMBER 19, 1959

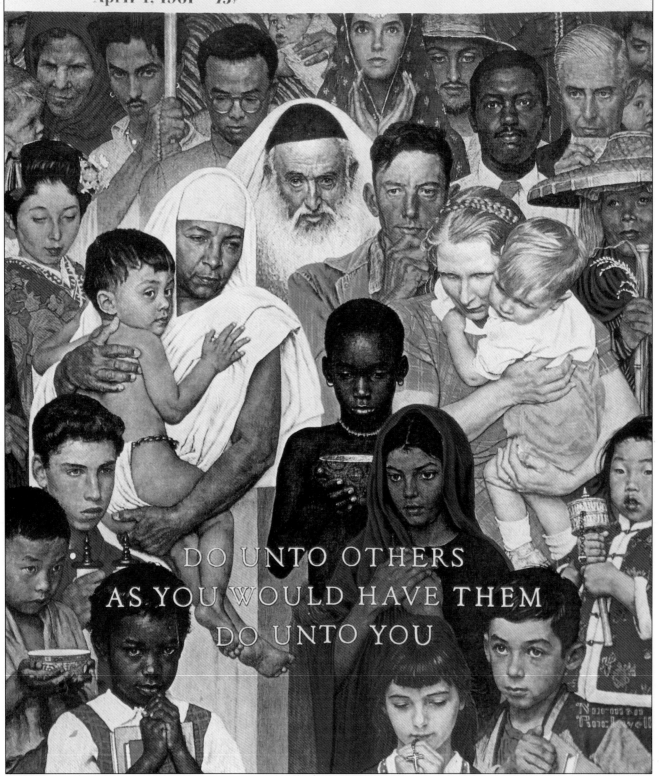

The Saturday Evening

POST

April 1, 1961 - *15¢*

THE NEW UTAH

My Adventures Among the U.S. Senators
By DEAN ACHESON

DO UNTO OTHERS
AS YOU WOULD HAVE THEM
DO UNTO YOU

Norman Rockwell
APRIL 1, 1961

THE SIXTIES AND AFTER

In the spring of 1961, the Curtis Corporation announced that Ben Hibbs, *Post* editor since 1942, would be replaced by Robert Fuoss, the current managing editor. This announcement ushered in a period of turmoil for the magazine and indeed for the Curtis Corporation itself.

The decision to replace Hibbs was part of a desperate effort to stem what the press characterized as "a relentless slump," a falling off of advertising revenue that had begun as far back as 1951.* Throughout the 1950s, while the *Post* celebrated prosperity, it had been struggling to recapture its former economic stability, but this was a different world from the one in which the *Post*

Time, August 4, 1961.

had achieved its ascendancy. Competition from more modern magazines as well as from radio and television took its toll, and while circulation was formidable, reaching 6,377,367 at the time when the replacement of Hibbs was announced, advertising profits continued to fall.*

The economic distress of the *Post* called not only for a new editor but for a new facelift as well. The cover of the *Post* had not been changed since 1942, and the Curtis Corporation saw modernization as urgent. Herb Lubalin, a well-known graphic designer, was hired, and his new design appeared on the September 16 cover for 1961. Now the word "POST," which had long stood on the upper left of the cover, was stretched across the entire top of the page, with the words "The Saturday Evening" placed inside the "O." But this facelift notwithstanding, the *Post* continued to straddle the old and the new, and it was Norman Rockwell who painted the first illustration for the renovated cover. With his back to us, a designer sits facing a drafting table on which are copies of the *Post* recording all the different logos back to the beginning of the century. The designer, as if examining it, displays the new logo.

The cover illustration for the new-look *Post* was subtly reminiscent of one of Rockwell's most famous covers, his triple self-portrait, which appeared on February 13, 1960 (page 264). Again with his back to us is the illustrator, Norman Rockwell, realistically rendered. He looks in a mirror that reflects his face and paints a canvas that reduces the realism as it enhances a kind of quiet intellectual nobility. Markedly, the spectacles Rockwell wears are reflected, eyeless, in the mirror, and altogether eliminated in the portrait. And tacked to the upper left of the easel are reproductions of famous self-portraits, among them those of Rembrandt and van Gogh.

The basic construction of the two paintings is strikingly similar, but the figure in each is treated quite differently. The wry irony of the triple self-portrait has vanished in the picture of the designer; that man is young, vigorous, and handsome, a nicely displayed expression of the vaunted new vigor of the *Post*.

The modernized *Post* may have used Rockwell for its first issue, but Rockwell's tenure on the magazine was reaching its end. He had done a small number of covers in the beginning of the decade in which he displayed his craftmanship to remarkably fine effect. A 1960 cover presents a repairman working on a church window. The repairman is rendered in typical Rockwell fashion, but he is painted in front of a brilliantly colored and elegantly executed stained glass window (April 16, 1960; page 268). And in "Connoisseur," a gray-suited gentleman, his back to us, regards a large modern painting, a Rockwell version of a Jackson Pollock (January 13, 1962; page 269). For the April 1, 1961, cover, Rockwell did "The Golden Rule," portraits of some two dozen people of all ages and ethnicities (page 258).

But the *Post* had come to favor his portraits. Indeed, under Fuoss's brief editorship, only his portraits were accepted. Besides the now-familiar portraits of presidential candidates in 1960, Rockwell also painted such diverse personalities as Jawaharlal Nehru and Jack Benny (January 1 and March 2, 1963). And then, in 1963, after forty-seven years, Norman Rockwell left the *Saturday Evening Post* for *Look* magazine. His last cover for the *Post* appeared on the

Time, May 19, 1961.

May 25, 1963, issue, a portrait of Gamal Abdel Nasser, president of Egypt.

The new logo, like the new editor, was short-lived, lasting only into mid-June 1962, after which time the former logo reappeared. The covers, however, underwent significant change. Like Rockwell, the other familiar *Post* cover artists were disappearing. In fact, cover art itself was quickly vanishing, replaced by photographic covers, which were soon used almost exclusively.

For the most part, the photographs on the covers of the *Post* served the idea of celebrity. Stories about celebrities had been an important feature of the magazine as early as the 1920s, but with the shift from cover art to photography by the mid-1960s, celebrity seemed to become the most significant aspect of the *Post*. To be sure, celebrity in America embraces a wide variety of persons. A selection from 1964 and 1965 includes Lady Bird Johnson, the Beatles, Eisenhower, Jill St. John, Harry S. Truman, Richard Burton, the Beatles (again), Malcolm X, Barry Goldwater, Lyndon Johnson, Bobby Kennedy, Jack Kennedy, J. Edgar Hoover, and the reigning Miss America.

By the middle of the decade, the cover of the *Post*, under the aegis of modernization, had, ironically enough, returned to its earliest format and its original purpose. In 1899, when editor Lorimer began to fit his magazine with covers, he often used photographs. And in the first years of the century, Lorimer selected covers that served to illustrate a featured article or piece of fiction. After more than a half century of independent illustration, the cover art, now most often a photograph, served to advertise a major article.

What had disappeared from the covers of the *Post* was twofold. First, no longer were the covers representations of America.

Certainly, those representations had been varied and various—sentimental, ironic, humorous, nostalgic—but through these images the *Post* had made a statement and shared with its readers what Americans thought America was all about. And second, along with those images went the primary function of the cover: a sign of, an identification of, the *Saturday Evening Post* itself.

The decade of the sixties saw the demise of the old *Post*. Editors came and went; the Curtis Corporation took on one president and then another; the *Post* was moved to New York; operating losses were staggering. Economy measures were instituted: several thousand employees were let go; the *Post* began, at first seasonally and then in general, biweekly publication. But the end could be postponed only so long. The last issue of the *Saturday Evening Post* appeared February 8, 1969.

The end of the *Post* was news, and more than that. There were feature stories in other magazines. In November 1969, Don A. Schanche wrote for *Esquire* "We Call on The Saturday Evening Post—For the Last Time," and the same month Michael M. Mooney did "The Death of the Post" for the *Atlantic Monthly*. That article included Norman Rockwell's own obituary: a painting of Ben Franklin, a tear dropping down his melancholy face. *Newsweek* carried "Requiem for the Post" by Stewart Alsop, who had written his first piece for the magazine fifty-three years earlier. Alsop blamed the death on television, and the consequent demise of the written word. But Mooney was surely more on target, understanding that in over half a century the world had greatly changed: "When Lorimer began, the hit song was 'School Days/ School Days.' On the day Martin S. Ackerman became president of Curtis [April

1968], 'Mrs. Robinson' was on the top of the charts. Sensible men will notice the difference."

The *Saturday Evening Post*, however, was destined for a second life. In the fall of 1970, Beurt SerVaas, then the president and principal stockholder of the reorganized Curtis Publishing Company, announced that he would resurrect the *Saturday Evening Post*. As far as the business of journalism went, SerVaas did not intend to emulate the old *Post*. His magazine would not be published weekly, but would appear at first as a quarterly and, if things went well, later on a monthly or bimonthly basis. Circulation would be strictly limited, with a target of 500,000, and costs would be met not by advertising but by the price of the magazine, estimated at somewhere between one and two dollars an issue.

But SerVaas did intend to emulate other characteristics of the *Post*, chiefly its representation of American life and values. The new magazine, to be edited by his wife, Cory, would include not only original materials but stories and articles that had previously appeared in the magazine. The *Post*, he said, "will be a patriotic magazine" and "will represent middle-America." And, once again, Norman Rockwell was called on. Rockwell, SerVaas informed the press, would do the first cover; "I hope it will be the most nostalgic drawing he has ever done." Moreover, SerVaas added, the new magazine would be what the old *Post* was best remembered for: in Rockwell's words, "kindness, sympathy, nostalgia, and optimism."*

The new *Post*—dated Summer 1971—appeared on the newsstands on June 1, 1971, a 160-page issue in a printing of 550,000. The graceful old logo, abandoned

Newsweek, November 16, 1970; *Time*, November 16, 1970.

in 1942, had been restored. The promised Rockwell cover, however, did not materialize, though the magazine managed to provide the next best thing. The Moffett Studios of Chicago took a Rockwell-esque photograph of Rockwell, seated in a chair and looking at his model—a small boy with an old *Post*-boy canvas bag across his shoulders. Behind, on an easel, is a drawing of the boy. Below is the announcement of an article, "A Visit with Norman Rockwell."

SerVaas did manage to feature the work of familiar *Post* cover artists for both the fall and the winter issues that year. George Hughes painted a version of generational differences, with sixties-style hippies in an antique car and ecology stickers and older folks in an imposing red convertible with vanity plates. John Philip Falter did a rural scene for the winter issue.

For the next two years the *Post* covers continued to trade in nostalgia, sometimes reprinting an old Rockwell cover and sometimes presenting new interpretations of familiar Rockwell works. Robert Charles Howe, who had won the magazine's Norman Rockwell contest, had his winning entry on the cover for March/April 1973: the artist at his easel, with Rockwell-like spectacles and pipe, and in the lower right a picture of the October 8, 1938, *Post*, with Rockwell's well-known cover illustration, "Deadline," which shows the artist, his back to the viewer, seated baffled before an empty canvas. Howe also did a reinterpretation of Rockwell's famous "Freedom from Want" for the November/December cover that same year. But the future of the cover for the new *Post* was not to lie in illustration.

That future was clearly signaled in the January/February issue for 1974, a photograph of Henry Kissinger by Richard Nixon's own photographer, Ollie Atkins.

Photography would once again come to dominate the cover. In the two decades since Kissinger's picture appeared, the new *Post* has most frequently featured photographs of celebrities from the worlds of politics and entertainment. The cover photo, moreover, serves to advertise a major article in the issue. There is some variation provided, both by original art and by occasional reprints of covers by both Rockwell and Leyendecker, powerful reminders of the achievements of American illustration and the vast reservoir of public affection for the *Saturday Evening Post*.

Norman Rockwell
OCTOBER 29, 1960

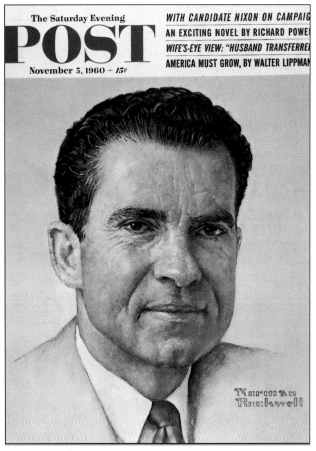

Norman Rockwell
NOVEMBER 5, 1960

The Saturday Evening POST

February 13, 1960 15¢

Beginning in this issue

AMERICA'S BEST LOVED ARTIST FINALLY TELLS HIS OWN STORY

NORMAN ROCKWELL

My Adventures As An Illustrator

By Norman Rockwell

Norman Rockwell
FEBRUARY 13, 1960

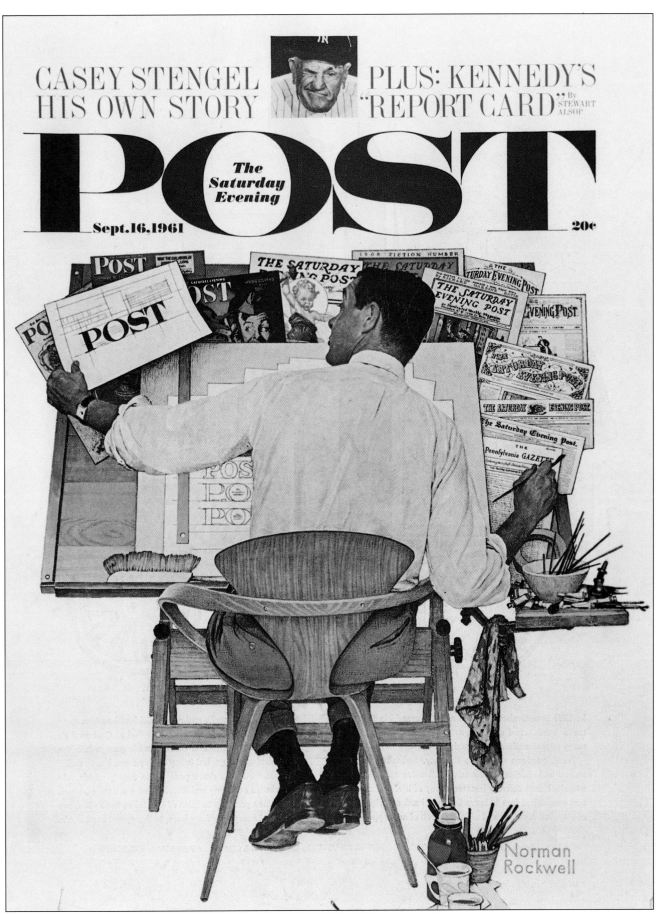

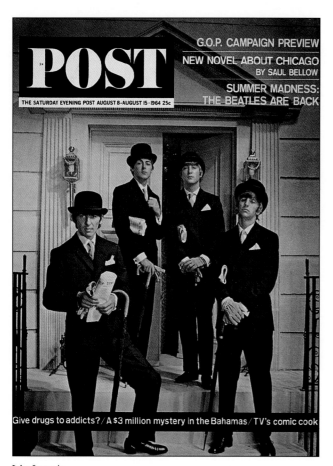

John Launois
AUGUST 8, 1964

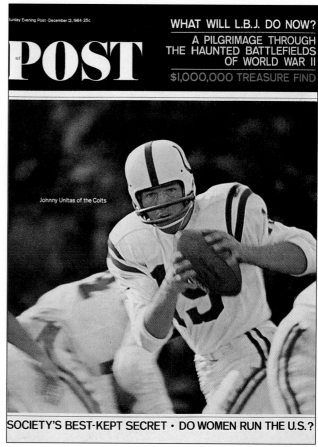

Neil Leifer
DECEMBER 12, 1964

John Zimmerman
FEBRUARY 22, 1964

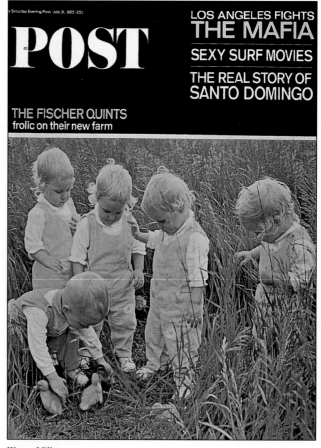

Wayne Miller
JULY 31, 1965

Larry Fried
OCTOBER 31, 1964

Burt Glinn
FEBRUARY 15, 1964

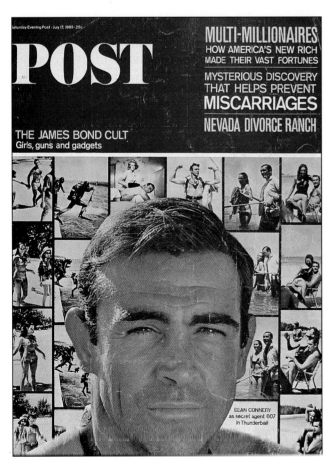

Pierluigi & Loomis Dean
JULY 17, 1965

John Launois
SEPTEMBER 12, 1964

The Saturday Evening **POST**

April 16, 1960 – 15¢

Perle Mesta TELLS HER OWN STORY:
THEY CALL ME MADAM

I CALL ON
JACK LEMMON
By Pete Martin

Norman Rockwell
APRIL 16, 1960

Norman Rockwell
JANUARY 13, 1962

Ben Prins
JANUARY 2, 1960

George Hughes
JANUARY 9, 1960

Stanley Meltzoff
JANUARY 16, 1960

James Williamson
JANUARY 23, 1960

Amos Sewell
JANUARY 30, 1960

John Clymer
FEBRUARY 6, 1960

Thornton Utz
FEBRUARY 20, 1960

George Hughes
FEBRUARY 27, 1960

Richard Sargent
MARCH 5, 1960

George Hughes
MARCH 12, 1960

John Falter
MARCH 19, 1960

George Hughes
MARCH 26, 1960

John Clymer
APRIL 2, 1960

Ben Prins
APRIL 9, 1960

Richard Sargent
APRIL 23, 1960

George Hughes
APRIL 30, 1960

John Falter
MAY 7, 1960

Richard Sargent
MAY 14, 1960

John Clymer
MAY 21, 1960

George Hughes
MAY 28, 1960

Thornton Utz
JUNE 4, 1960

George Hughes
JUNE 11, 1960

Thornton Utz
JUNE 18, 1960

John Falter
JUNE 25, 1960

Constantin Alajalov
JULY 2, 1960

John Clymer
JULY 9, 1960

James Williamson
JULY 16, 1960

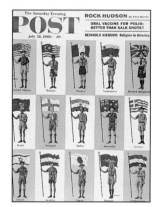

James Lewicki
JULY 23, 1960

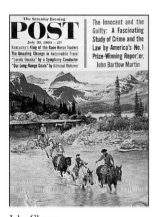

John Clymer
JULY 30, 1960

George Hughes
AUGUST 6, 1960

Amos Sewell
AUGUST 13, 1960

Ben Prins
AUGUST 20, 1960

271

Norman Rockwell
AUGUST 27, 1960

Richard Sargent
SEPTEMBER 3, 1960

Thornton Utz
SEPTEMBER 10, 1960

Norman Rockwell
SEPTEMBER 17, 1960

George Hughes
SEPTEMBER 24, 1960

Constantin Alajalov
OCTOBER 1, 1960

Lonie Bee
OCTOBER 8, 1960

John Falter
OCTOBER 15, 1960

Richard Sargent
OCTOBER 22, 1960

Constantin Alajalov
NOVEMBER 12, 1960

George Hughes
NOVEMBER 19, 1960

Amos Sewell
NOVEMBER 26, 1960

Richard Sargent
DECEMBER 3, 1960

George Hughes
DECEMBER 10, 1960

Ben Prins
DECEMBER 17, 1960

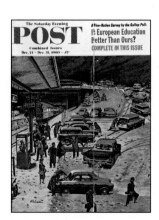

Ben Prins
DECEMBER 24, 1960

John Falter
JANUARY 7, 1961

James Williamson
JANUARY 14, 1961

John Atherton
JANUARY 21, 1961

Earl Mayan
JANUARY 28, 1961

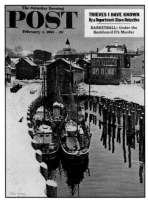

John Clymer
FEBRUARY 4, 1961

George Hughes
FEBRUARY 11, 1961

Richard Sargent
FEBRUARY 18, 1961

Ben Prins
FEBRUARY 25, 1961

Constantin Alajalov
MARCH 4, 1961

M. Coburn Whitmore
MARCH 11, 1961

John Clymer
MARCH 18, 1961

George Hughes
MARCH 25, 1961

Constantin Alajalov
APRIL 8, 1961

John Clymer
APRIL 15, 1961

George Hughes
APRIL 22, 1961

Amos Sewell
APRIL 29, 1961

Kurt Ard
MAY 6, 1961

John Falter
MAY 13, 1961

Thornton Utz
MAY 20, 1961

John Clymer
MAY 27, 1961

Constantin Alajalov
JUNE 3, 1961

Amos Sewell
JUNE 10, 1961

Richard Sargent
JUNE 17, 1961

Ben Prins
JUNE 24, 1961

John Falter
JULY 1, 1961

Ben Prins
JULY 8, 1961

George Hughes
JULY 15, 1961

Thornton Utz
JULY 22, 1961

John Clymer
JULY 29, 1961

Ben Prins
AUGUST 5, 1961

Constantin Alajalov
AUGUST 12, 1961

George Hughes
AUGUST 19, 1961

Richard Sargent
AUGUST 26, 1961

George Hughes
SEPTEMBER 2, 1961

John Clymer
SEPTEMBER 9, 1961

John Falter
SEPTEMBER 23, 1961

Constantin Alajalov
SEPTEMBER 30, 1961

John Falter
OCTOBER 7, 1961

Herb Lubalin
OCTOBER 14, 1961

Richard Sargent
OCTOBER 21, 1961

John Falter
OCTOBER 28, 1961

Thornton Utz
NOVEMBER 4, 1961

George Hughes
NOVEMBER 11, 1961

Elliott Erwitt
NOVEMBER 18, 1961

Norman Rockwell
NOVEMBER 25, 1961

John Falter
DECEMBER 2, 1961

Burt Glinn
DECEMBER 9, 1961

Richard Sargent
DECEMBER 16, 1961

Bill Bridges
DECEMBER 23, 1961

Gyo Fujikawa
JANUARY 6, 1962

John Bryson
JANUARY 20, 1962

George Hughes
JANUARY 27, 1962

John Falter
FEBRUARY 3, 1962

Amos Sewell
FEBRUARY 10, 1962

Constantin Alajalov
FEBRUARY 17, 1962

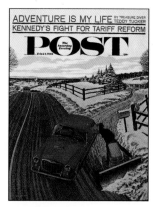

James Williamson
FEBRUARY 24, 1962

Richard Sargent
MARCH 3, 1962

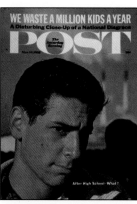

Wayne Miller
MARCH 10, 1962

John Falter
MARCH 17, 1962

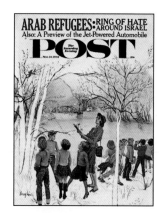

George Hughes
MARCH 24, 1962

Richard Sargent
MARCH 31, 1962

Constantin Alajalov
APRIL 7, 1962

John Bryson
APRIL 14, 1962

Richard Sargent
APRIL 21, 1962

James Williamson
APRIL 28, 1962

John Clymer
MAY 5, 1962

Constantin Alajalov
MAY 12, 1962

Ben Prins
MAY 19, 1962

George Hughes
MAY 26, 1962

Richard Sargent
JUNE 2, 1962

Ben Prins
JUNE 9, 1962

Eric Carpenter
JUNE 16, 1962

George Hughes
JUNE 23, 1962

Constantin Alajalov
JUNE 30, 1962

George Hughes
JULY 14, 1962

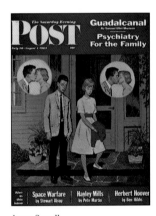

Amos Sewell
JULY 28, 1962

Edward Clark
AUGUST 11, 1962

Amos Sewell
AUGUST 25, 1962

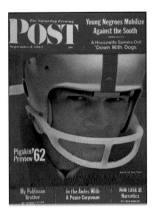

Gordon Tenney
SEPTEMBER 8, 1962

John Falter
SEPTEMBER 15, 1962

Erik Blegvard
SEPTEMBER 22, 1962

James Williamson
SEPTEMBER 29, 1962

Yousuf Karsh
OCTOBER 6, 1962

Robert McCall
OCTOBER 13, 1962

John Clymer
OCTOBER 20, 1962

James Williamson
OCTOBER 27, 1962

Norman Rockwell
NOVEMBER 3, 1962

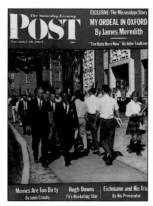

John Burns
NOVEMBER 10, 1962

Thornton Utz
NOVEMBER 17, 1962

Jan Balet
NOVEMBER 24, 1962

Constantin Alajalov
DECEMBER 1, 1962

Sam Dion
DECEMBER 8, 1962

Larry Fried
DECEMBER 15, 1962

Wayne Miller
DECEMBER 22, 1962

Frank Mullins
JANUARY 5, 1963

Norman Rockwell
JANUARY 19, 1963

Larry Fried
JANUARY 26, 1963

Allan Grant
FEBRUARY 2, 1963

Bill Whittingham
FEBRUARY 9, 1963

Burt Glinn
FEBRUARY 16, 1963

Marshall Hawkins
FEBRUARY 23, 1963

Norman Rockwell
MARCH 2, 1963

Mark Kauffman
MARCH 9, 1963

Burt Glinn
MARCH 16, 1963

Jerry Rose
MARCH 23, 1963

John Bryson
MARCH 30, 1963

Norman Rockwell
APRIL 6, 1963

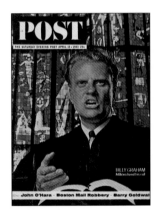

John Zimmerman
APRIL 13, 1963

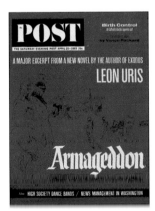

Feliks Topolski
APRIL 20, 1963

Ollie Atkins
APRIL 27, 1963

Lawrence J. Schiller
MAY 4, 1963

Lawrence J. Schiller
MAY 11, 1963

John Zimmerman
MAY 18, 1963

Norman Rockwell
MAY 25, 1963

Bert Stern
JUNE 1, 1963

David Passalacqua
JUNE 8, 1963

John Launois
JUNE 15, 1963

Martin Lederhandler
JUNE 22, 1963

John Bryson
JUNE 29, 1963

Lawrence J. Schiller
JULY 13, 1963

David Passalacqua
JULY 27, 1963

Louis Glanzman
AUGUST 10, 1963

Bob Huntzinger
AUGUST 24, 1963

Allan Grant
SEPTEMBER 7, 1963

Burt Glinn
SEPTEMBER 14, 1963

John Zimmerman
SEPTEMBER 21, 1963

Burt Glinn
SEPTEMBER 28, 1963

Lawrence J. Schiller
OCTOBER 5, 1963

John Zimmerman
OCTOBER 12, 1963

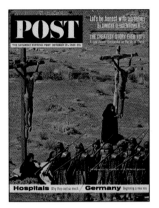

John Launois
OCTOBER 19, 1963

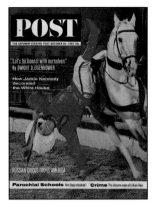

Burt Glinn
OCTOBER 26, 1963

Philippe Halsman
NOVEMBER 2, 1963

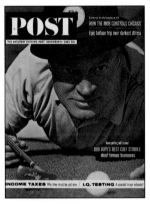

Artist unknown
NOVEMBER 9, 1963

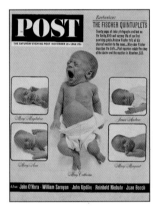

John Zimmerman
NOVEMBER 16, 1963

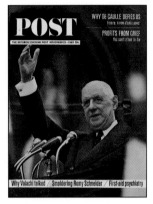

John Launois
NOVEMBER 23, 1963

Artist unknown
NOVEMBER 30, 1963

Allan Grant
DECEMBER 7, 1963

Norman Rockwell
DECEMBER 14, 1963

John Launois
DECEMBER 21, 1963

Elgin Ciampi
JANUARY 4, 1964

Lynn Pelham
JANUARY 18, 1964

Burt Glinn
JANUARY 25, 1964

Inge Morath
FEBRUARY 1, 1964

Mark Kauffman
FEBRUARY 8, 1964

281

Jack Fields
FEBRUARY 29, 1964

David Douglas Duncan
MARCH 7, 1964

John Launois
MARCH 14, 1964

John Zimmerman
MARCH 21, 1964

Burt Glinn
MARCH 28, 1964

Philippe Halsman
APRIL 4, 1964

Lawrence J. Schiller
APRIL 11, 1964

Lawrence J. Schiller
APRIL 18, 1964

John Zimmerman
APRIL 25, 1964

John Zimmerman
MAY 2, 1964

Frank Bez
MAY 9, 1964

Harry Redl
MAY 16, 1964

John Zimmerman
MAY 23, 1964

John Launois
MAY 30, 1964

Henry Ries
JUNE 6, 1964

John Launois
JUNE 13, 1964

Lawrence J. Schiller
JUNE 20, 1964

John Launois
JUNE 27, 1964

John Weiner
JULY 11, 1964

Jack Fields
JULY 25, 1964

John Zimmerman
AUGUST 22, 1964

Robert Barth
SEPTEMBER 5, 1964

John Zimmerman
SEPTEMBER 19, 1964

John Zimmerman
SEPTEMBER 26, 1964

Lawrence J. Schiller
OCTOBER 3, 1964

Lawrence J. Schiller
OCTOBER 10, 1964

John Launois
OCTOBER 17, 1964

Burt Glinn
OCTOBER 24, 1964

Lynn Pelham
NOVEMBER 7, 1964

Edward Behr
NOVEMBER 14, 1964

Ken Danvers
NOVEMBER 21, 1964

Burt Glinn
NOVEMBER 28, 1964

John Bryson
DECEMBER 5, 1964

Mark Kauffman
DECEMBER 26, 1964

Bob Willoughby
JANUARY 16, 1965

Lynn Pelham
JANUARY 30, 1965

Mark Kauffman
FEBRUARY 13, 1965

Burt Glinn
FEBRUARY 27, 1965

N. M. Bodecker
MARCH 13, 1965

Burt Glinn
MARCH 27, 1965

Lawrence J. Schiller
APRIL 10, 1965

Wayne Miller
APRIL 24, 1965

P. Orlando
MAY 8, 1965

John Zimmerman
MAY 22, 1965

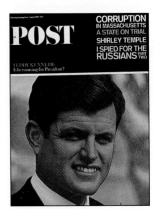

Ted Polumbaum
JUNE 5, 1965

John Launois
JUNE 19, 1965

Ken Heyman
JULY 3, 1965

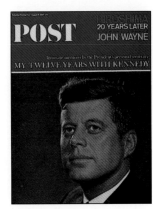

Yousuf Karsh
AUGUST 14, 1965

John Launois
AUGUST 28, 1965

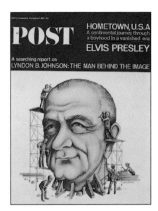

Blake Hampton
SEPTEMBER 11, 1965

Fred Ward
SEPTEMBER 25, 1965

Bob Willoughby
OCTOBER 9, 1965

Jean L. Huens
OCTOBER 23, 1965

Len Steckler
NOVEMBER 6, 1965

Wayne Miller
NOVEMBER 20, 1965

Dan Wynn
DECEMBER 4, 1965

Wayne Miller
DECEMBER 18, 1965

Blake Hampton
JANUARY 1, 1966

Hiro
JANUARY 15, 1966

Philippe Halsman
JANUARY 29, 1966

Maurie Rosen
FEBRUARY 12, 1966

John Launois
FEBRUARY 26, 1966

Fred Otner
MARCH 12, 1966

Lorry Fried & Nninl Kingel
MARCH 26, 1966

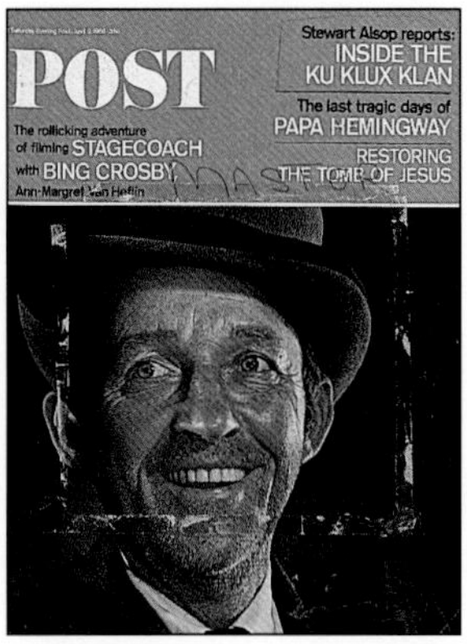

Philippe Halsman
APRIL 9, 1966

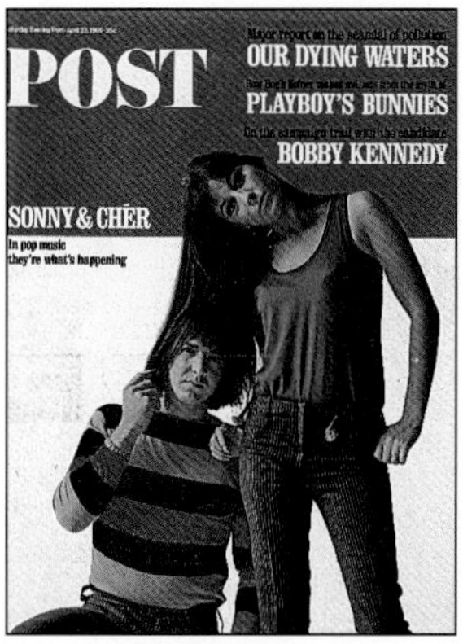

Jerry Schatzberg
APRIL 23, 1966

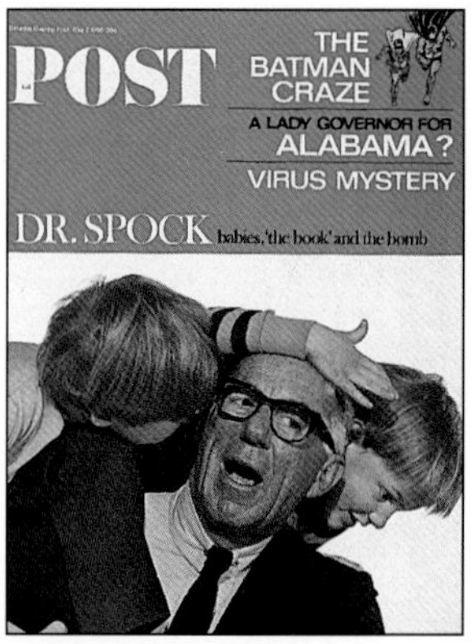

Philippe Halsman
MAY 7, 1966

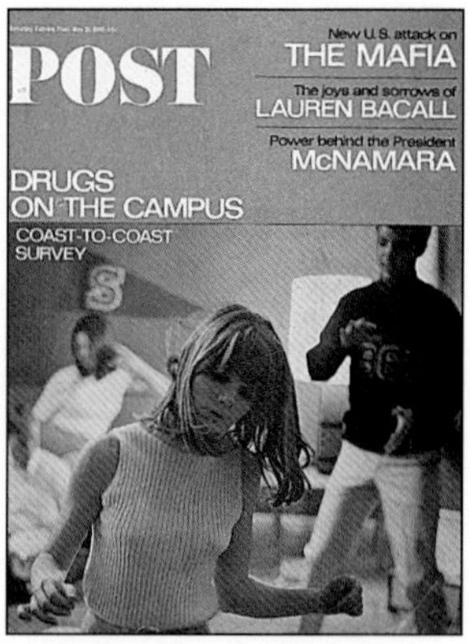

Carl Fischer
MAY 21, 1966

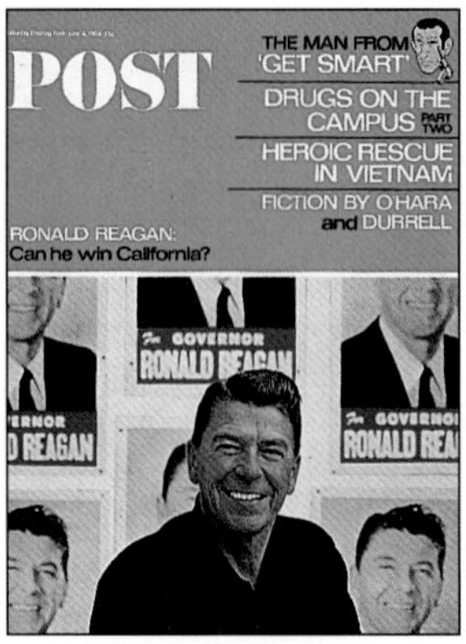

Jack Fields
JUNE 4, 1966

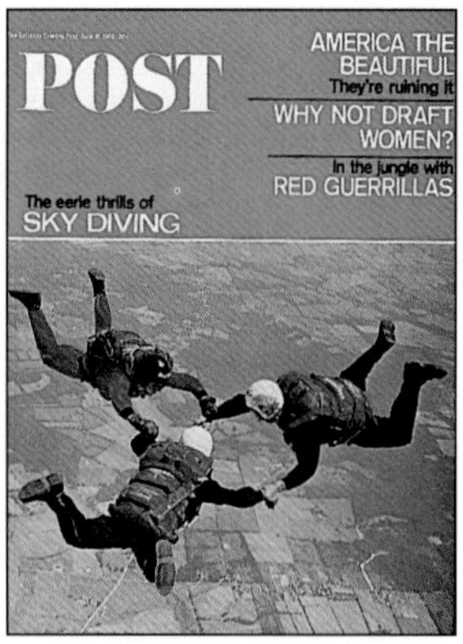

Jerry Irwin
JUNE 18, 1966

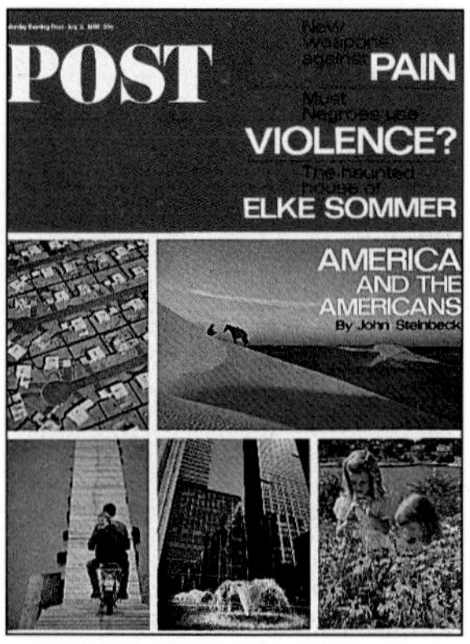

Artist unknown
JULY 2, 1966

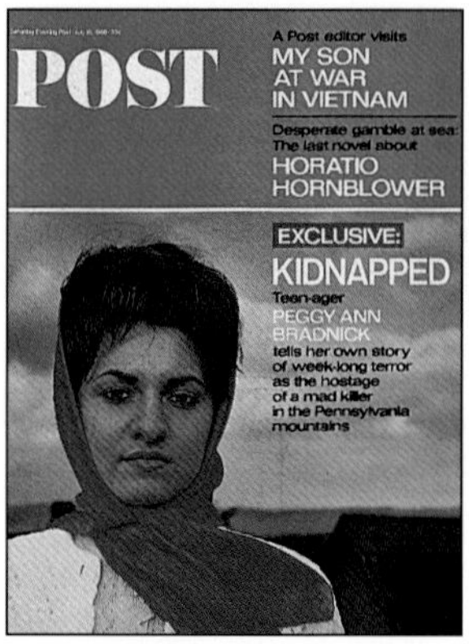

Harvey Lloyd
JULY 16, 1966

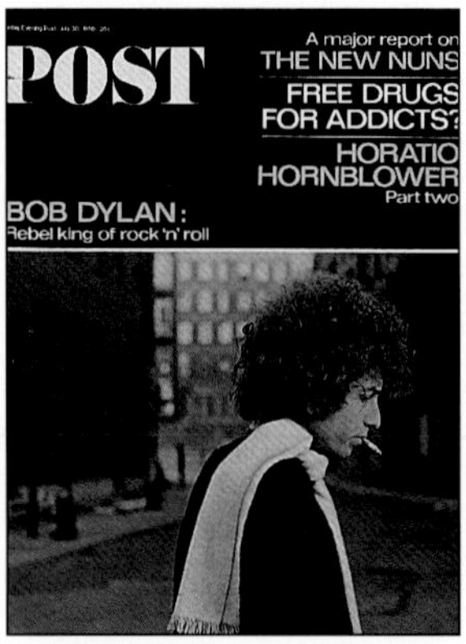

Jerry Schatzberg
JULY 30, 1966

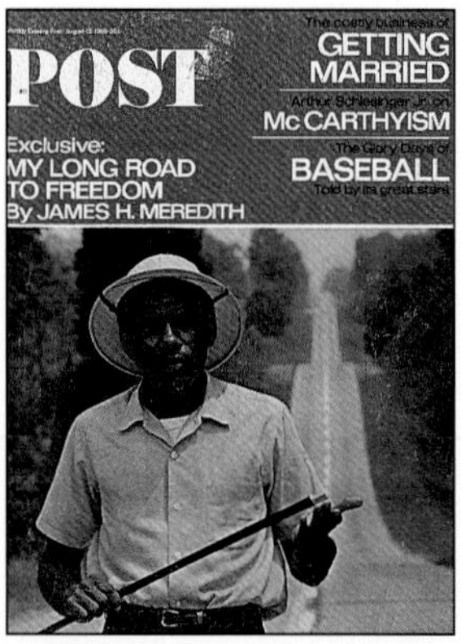

Matt Herron
AUGUST 13, 1966

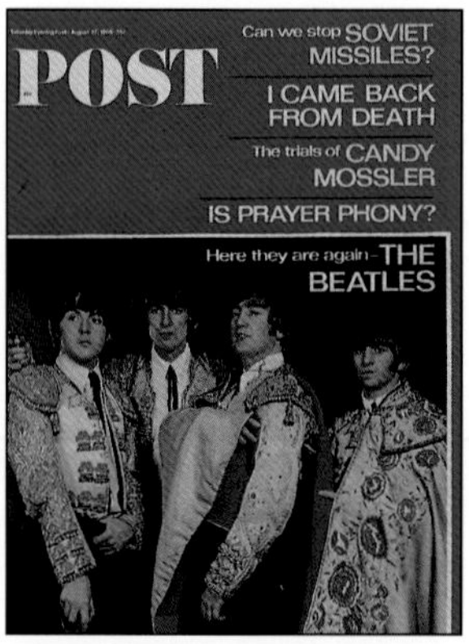

Bill Francis
AUGUST 27, 1966

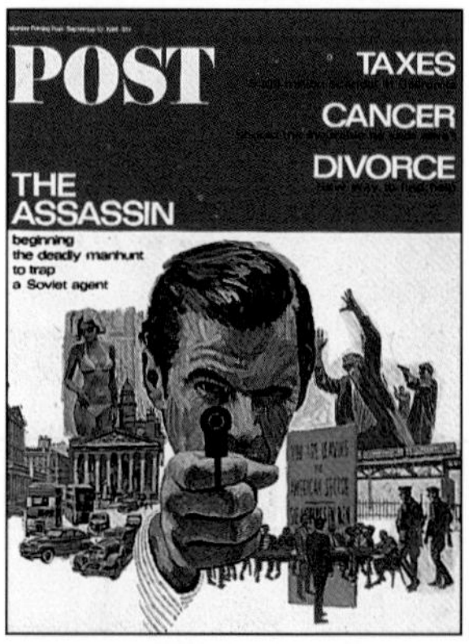

Mitchell Hooks
SEPTEMBER 10, 1966

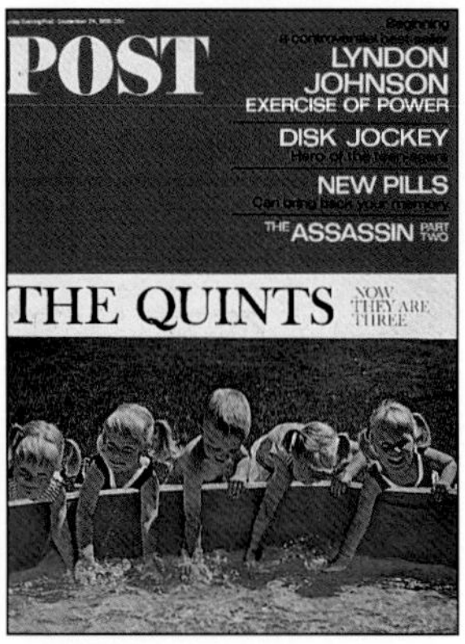

Suzanne Szasz
SEPTEMBER 24, 1966

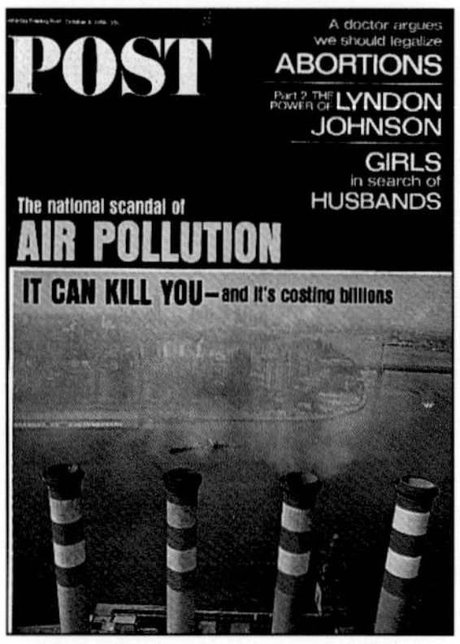

John Launois
OCTOBER 8, 1966

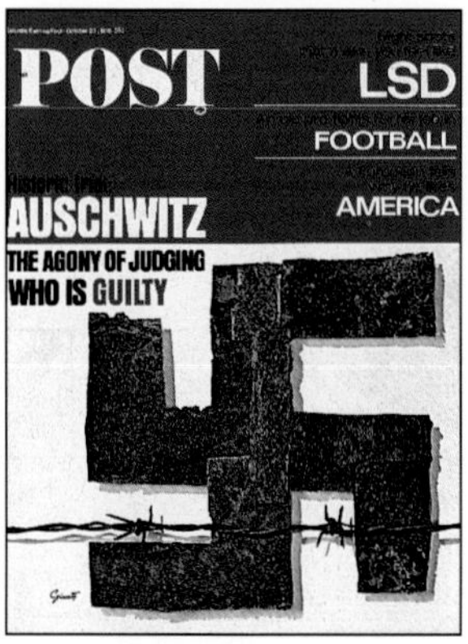

George Giusti
OCTOBER 22, 1966

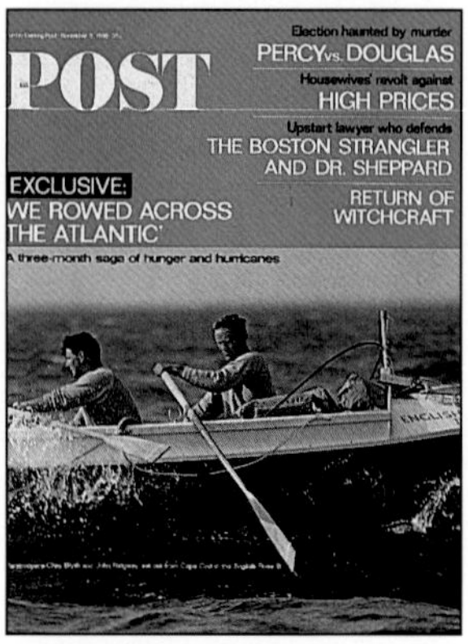

Fred Kaplan
NOVEMBER 5, 1966

Philippe Halsman
NOVEMBER 19, 1966

Paul Ronald
DECEMBER 3, 1966

Paul Calle
DECEMBER 17, 1966

Dan Wynn
DECEMBER 31, 1966

Fred Otnes
JANUARY 14, 1967

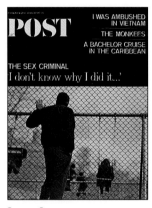

Jacques Lowe
JANUARY 28, 1967

Charles Moore
FEBRUARY 11, 1967

Charles Moore
FEBRUARY 25, 1967

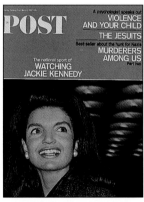

Irv Steinberg
MARCH 11, 1967

Dan Wynn
MARCH 25, 1967

Austin Briggs
APRIL 8, 1967

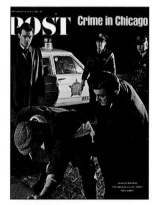

Declan Haun
APRIL 22, 1967

Fred Otnes
MAY 6, 1967

John Launois
MAY 20, 1967

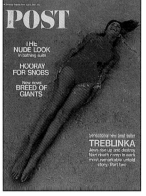

Ron Harris
JUNE 3, 1967

Don Ornitz
JUNE 17, 1967

287

Ray Burley & David Attie
JULY 1, 1967

Frank and Nancy Sinatra,
Supremes - photo
JULY 15, 1967

Matt Herron
JULY 29, 1967

Jacques Lowe
AUGUST 12, 1967

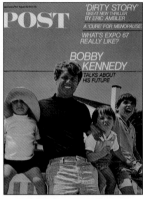

Philippe Halsman
AUGUST 26, 1967

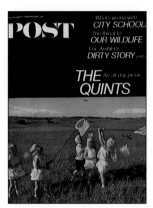

John Launois
SEPTEMBER 9, 1967

Golsong
SEPTEMBER 23, 1967

John Launois
OCTOBER 7, 1967

M-G-M
OCTOBER 21, 1967

John Launois
NOVEMBER 4, 1967

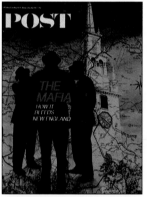

David Attie
NOVEMBER 18, 1967

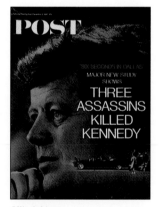

Ollie Atkins
DECEMBER 2, 1967

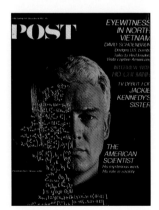

John Launois
DECEMBER 16, 1967

Robert Weber
DECEMBER 30, 1967

Ollie Atkins & David Attie
JANUARY 13, 1968

Fred Ward
JANUARY 27, 1968

Ronald Searle
FEBRUARY 10, 1968

Milton H. Green
FEBRUARY 24, 1968

David Attie
MARCH 9, 1968

Steve Schapiro
MARCH 23, 1968

Eula Greene
APRIL 6, 1968

Fred Ward
APRIL 20, 1968

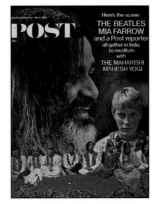

Marvin Lichtner & Larry Kurland
MAY 4, 1968

Don Ornitz
MAY 18, 1968

Steve Schapiro
JUNE 1, 1968

Vernon Merritt III & Dan McCoy
JUNE 15, 1968

Charles Moore
JUNE 29, 1968

Charles Moore
JUNE 29, 1968

Charles Moore
JULY 13, 1968

Charles Moore
JULY 13, 1968

Charles Moore
JULY 27, 1968

Charles Moore
JULY 27, 1968

Jon Naar
AUGUST 10, 1968

John Huehnergarth
AUGUST 24, 1968

Jerry Schatzberg
SEPTEMBER 7, 1968

Paul Calle
SEPTEMBER 21, 1968

J. Edward Bailey
OCTOBER 5, 1968

John Launois
OCTOBER 19, 1968

Elliott Landy
NOVEMBER 2, 1968

Kim Massie
NOVEMBER 16, 1968

Don Ornitz
NOVEMBER 30, 1968

Gene Holtan
DECEMBER 14, 1968

United Church Press
DECEMBER 28, 1968

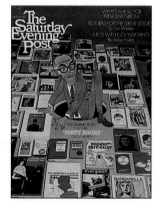

Aurelius Battaglia &
Karl-Heinz Schumacher
JANUARY 25, 1969

Charles Moore
FEBRUARY 8, 1969

INDEX